Shakespeare Short Guides

Much Ado About Nothing

analysis, notes and exemplar essays

E.N Cartwright

DEDICATION

To my partner: the great listener.

CONTENTS

ACKNOWLEDGMENTS

All my students, who have taught me as much for this as I have taught them.

Introduction

What's expected of me in this exam?

Well, hello, exam candidate.

I'm sure you've bought this purely to help you understand Shakespeare just a little better and not, of course, to cram an exemplar essay into your head a few days before the exam. Eek!

Now, the first thing to remember is that your teacher has given you specific advice for your exam, and she/he knows you much better than this book. So: FOLLOW THEIR ADVICE FIRST!

Do what they want you to do, take good notes, and listen to their feedback to improve. You have most likely had lots of attempts and feedback on your essay writing skills. Follow what your teacher wants you to do and use this guide to add to that.

Now, I have taught many kinds of exams to many pupils across many countries. Here is some general advice that I would bet applies to any exam:

- There is a time limit. It may be the Shakespeare is the only thing you need to do or part of a bigger paper, but you must manage your time fully.

- You must write a complete essay – something half-finished scores less than a short but finished essay.

- You must show knowledge of the whole text (beginning, middle and end) to score top marks. A marker wants to see that you understand it all.

- You must give **references** and **quotations**. These are the basis for any response.

- You should name **techniques** of English Lit (metaphor, simile, word choice, etc). This is usually in a mark scheme, looked for by markers.

- An introduction and a conclusion are rarely in a mark scheme but are expected in a longer piece of critical writing. If your exam doesn't call for a formal 'essay' then these may not to be needed but be guided by your teacher.

- The exam will usually provide a question/**task**. Sometimes tasks are genre specific and, so, you must choose 'Drama' since you are covering *Much Ado About Nothing* which is a play. Oh, and put the number of the question – this helps your marker.

- Don't write everything you know – choose what answers the task. Be selective, and don't just write a plot summary. That's not what a critical response is. Yes, show knowledge of what happens but a critical essay is something much more.

- The quickest way to do the above is to **repeat the key words** from the task itself. If it asks about a "character you feel sympathy for" then say the word "sympathy" at least twice a paragraph.

- There is no set 'way' to do an essay. You may have been taught TARTS, BAPs, PEAs, PEARs, PCQEs, and on and on, but it's rare for an exam board to have a preference.

  All these acronyms are just a teacher's way of trying to get you to do the following: show you know the play; show you know some quotations; show you know some analysis: and link all that information to the task give in the exam.

Much Ado About Nothing

Context

Who was Shakespeare and why did he write this rollercoaster play?

A writer whom English teachers love. He died a long time ago.

There's actually very little else you need to know about Shakespeare's actual life other than that. English Literature exams aren't testing you on your historical knowledge and English Literature mark scheme rarely reward this.

But sometimes **social and historical context** is in the mark scheme. This isn't the same as facts about Shakespeare. This is information about the setting, writer, or political/social climate at the time of the production of the drama which helps us understand it better or in a different way. This information is especially useful if you are looking for that A or top band mark.

So ...

Much Ado About Nothing is a comedy. For a modern audience, this means 'funny', and this is true: the play is meant to be laughed at and has jokes, though some of these jokes need a bit of explaining to be understood. But it is also a **Shakespearean comedy**. What does this mean? Well, it has no death and ends in a marriage; it has something ultimately like a 'happy' ending. These contrast with the **Shakespearean tragedies** which end in death, usually of the central characters. The line between **comedy** and **tragedy** in Shakespeare is very thin and often we don't know which we are getting until towards the end of the play. This can be seen in the fact that *Much Ado About Nothing* has a lot in common with *Romeo and Juliet* and follow similar patterns until *Much Ado* changes to become a comedy and *Romeo and Juliet* (spoiler alert!) a tragedy.

The play was written during the **Elizabethan era** (i.e. the reign of Queen Elizabeth the First). She was an avid supporter of the arts and theatre. In fact, she approved the building of the first public theatres in England! Having a powerful and unmarried Queen on the throne meant that gender, gender roles and marriage were all **zeitgeist** (important) topics of the time. Whether or not Queen Elizabeth was a virgin, who she would marry, and how powerful or masculine a female Prince (a word for a monarch, not necessarily a man) could be played in the Elizabethan psyche. Elizabeth refused to marry or produce children, an important part of her role as a woman and Queen yet was powerful and sparked a **renaissance** of English culture and power in Europe. Elizabeth's defiance of her gender was a major talking point in European politics of the time and Shakespeare reflects this in much of his writing, including in this play. It is also interesting to note that only men/boys were allowed to act on stage and, so, all female parts are played by men, though more often younger boys. This was another way in which gender was confused and muddled within this play – and, in fact, within all of Shakespeare's plays.

Now this **social and historical knowledge** isn't all that you need to know to understand the play – and, in fact, you could probably understand it quite well without knowing it – but it does add dimension and flavour to any critical response should you choose to include it. The use of this kind of information tends to be the marker of a higher end candidate as it shows a deepness of thought about *Much Ado About Nothing* that many other candidates lack, especially if you can weave it into your answer taking away from your knowledge of the play itself.

And that's the key: it's always extra!

The Text Itself

Remember it's a play!

Before we go much further you just need to remember one clear and distinct thing – this is a play/drama.

Why is that important?

Well, markers rarely see essays on Shakespeare that remember it is designed to be watched and not to be read. You get a few extra marks for understanding that idea. For example, acknowledging that there are actors, sets, special effects, stage directions, etc. These all show that you understand the **genre** of the thing that you have studied. This is rarely done and can make your essay stand out from the crowd.

These things also affect our understanding of the play. For example, almost all presentations of Hero as a character have her as quiet and demure. She doesn't have many lines and is meant to be the 'perfect' daughter and, so, often actresses play this character as wooden and even a little one dimensional. It is possible that Shakespeare wrote her this way! Yet, some actresses chose to play Hero as strong, powerful, and intelligent. This is a totally different interpretation of the same character.

Plays can change from how they seem to be written!

Common mistakes because it's a drama:

- The person who wrote it is Shakespeare, the writer, or the dramatist.

  It's **not** the poet or the maker, for example.

- The text is called the text, the play, or the drama.

  It is **not** the book or the film. You may have used a book or film to help you study the play, but you are writing an essay on the play.

- The audience or the viewer reacts.

  It is **not** the reader. You may have read sections of the play, but essays discuss influence on audience.

- You need to know the difference between **dialogue** and **stage directions**.

  - ✓ Dialogue: these are the words written on the page by Shakespeare and designed to be learned and said out-loud by the actors.

  - ✓ Stage directions: these are the instructions written by Shakespeare about sets, movement of actors, special effects. These are not meant to be reader to the audience, although you can analyse them in your essay.

    Shakespeare (because he directed his own plays) doesn't use many stage directions. He didn't need to write instructions down – he would just say them to the actors himself. They are usually printed on the page in *italics.*

The Plot and Characters

Eh, what happens?

Now, this is a very complicated play. A lot happens but, to cheer you up a bit, you don't need to know every line and every 'why' and every action. No exam board can expect you (only a student!) to have knowledge that many English Literature graduates do not have – especially as this is written in some of the most complicated language in history.

What they do expect is for you to have an overview understanding. They might not expect you to know what happens in Act 1 Scene 5 line 5, but they do expect you to know that Beatrice and Benedick once had a relationship and then end up together again the end of the play. These are fundamentals!

'Back of the book' summary

In Messina, the capital of Sicily, Don Pedro, and his soldiers (most notably Benedick and Claudio) arrive after successfully winning a war. Leonato, the governor of Messina, invites them to stay for a month to celebrate. This gives Hero the chance to fall in love with Claudio, and Benedick and Beatrice to pick up their "merry war" and light-hearted bickering … but lurking in the background is the "bastard" prince, Don Jon, with evil schemes to bring all this romantic happiness to "nothing".

The Main Cast

The Soldiers

Don Pedro, a prince

Benedick, a lord and long-time soldier/companion of Don Pedro

Claudio, a count and younger companion of Don Pedro

Don Jon, brother of Don Pedro and "bastard" Prince who started the war prior to the play

Borachio, follower of Don Jon

Conrad, follower of Don Jon

Court of Messina

Leonato, governor

Antonio, brother of Leonato

Hero, Leonato's daughter and heir

Beatrice, Hero's orphaned cousin and **ward** of Leonato

Margaret, waiting-women of Hero

Ursula, waiting-women of Hero

Others

Dogberry, comic character – constable of the night's watch

Verges, comic character – Dogberry's partner

Friar Francis, a priest

Sexton, a judge at the trial of Borachio

The Watch, the watchmen (police) of Messina

Act 1

The court of Messina are on stage and a messenger arrives to tell them that Don Pedro is on his way, having won his war again his illegitimate brother who wished to take his throne. Beatrice asks about Benedick, showing her interest in him from the start, although she covers it up.

Don Pedro, Claudio, and Benedick arrive with others (including Don Jon). Beatrice and Benedick, as promised, argue using **wit** – the Shakespearean force of mind and humour – and they seem equally matched, although Beatrice seems to get the better of Benedick here. Don Pedro announces that Leonato has given his men leave to stay for a month of celebrations.

All others leave the stage but Don Pedro, Claudio and Benedick who discuss the women they have met. Claudio is in love with Hero, Leonato's daughter, and establishes that Hero is Leonato's heir and she will inherit his month and position. Don Pedro agrees to act as an intermediary for the couple to arrange their marriage as he thinks they are a good match. This establishes that this play will be dominated by love and marriage, natural elements for soldiers just out of war.

Elsewhere Leonato and Antonio discuss the conversation about Hero, but it has been misheard. They think that Don Pedro is in love with Hero and wishes to propose for himself. This establishes the ideas of misunderstanding, gossip, overhearing and confusion that drive the narrative and much of the humour of the play. They are overjoyed as this would be an excellent match as he is a prince. They say they will tell Hero so she can prepare her answer – notice Hero has no choice in this matter!

In another part of Messina, Don Jon, and his friends, Borachio and Conrad, also discuss this conversation between Don Pedro and his men. Borachio also overheard the conversation, but he overheard it correctly – that Don Pedro is going to attempt to "woo" Hero for Claudio. Don Jon, who was pardoned for the war by his brother, has been pretending to be sorry but shows his friends (and the audience) that he wishes to be a villain and cause pain for Don Pedro using this information.

12

Act 2

A **masque** is to be held in celebration. This is a ball where masks are worn so we must be careful of who is speaking and who they are claiming to be! Hero has been instructed to accept Don Pedro's proposal of marriage should he ask. Various couples in masks form, for example Hero and Don Pedro. Benedick approaches Beatrice but refuses to say who he is. Beatrice immediately starts saying mean things about Benedick (it is unclear if she knows who she is speaking to) who gets upset. Don Jon and Borachio also find Claudio, whom they recognise, and ask if he is Benedick. Claudio nods. Don Jon claims Don Pedro is in love with Hero for himself but cannot be allowed to propose as she is not an equal match. Claudio is convinced his friend betrayed him.

All the characters come together again and remove their masks. Benedick goes off in anger at what has been said. Beatrice mentions they were once romantically involved, and he hurt her. Don Pedro announces the marriage of Hero and Claudio, arranged with Leonato. Don Jon's plan collapsed fast! Beatrice claims that everyone is getting married and leaving her. Don Pedro jokingly offers to marry her, but she turns him down. Once she leaves, the others decide they are going to trick Beatrice and Benedick into falling in love and getting married.

Later, Don Jon is furious his plan did not work. Borachio, his friend, comes up with a scheme where they will use Margaret's shape in Hero's bedroom window to make Claudio and Don Pedro think that Hero has a secret lover.

At the same time, Benedick is walking in Leonato's garden and claiming he will never fall in love like Claudio. He sees Claudio, Don Pedro and Leonato walking his way and hides. All the men see Benedick but pretend they did not – they are going to use this to trick him. They then have a pretend conversation which they know he will overhear in which they claim that Beatrice is love with Benedick but is too afraid to say it. In fact, they imply that her meanness to him is a sign of her love! They men go off, laughing at having tricked Benedick. This is called the

gulling scene. They make it clear the women will perform the same trick on Beatrice when they get the chance.

Benedick comes out of hiding and suddenly discusses being in love with Beatrice and wanting to marry her. Beatrice has been sent from the house to come and fetch Benedick for dinner, unaware that he thinks he loves her. She is exceptionally caustic and mean to him, which he takes as a sign of her hidden love. Beatrice notices that there is something off about Benedick but can't quite figure it out yet.

Act 3

The women (Hero, Ursula, and Margaret) perform the same trick on Beatrice. They are walking in the garden with Beatrice deliberately being goaded/manipulated by overhearing. This scene has some of the greatest chunks of lines for Hero, showing her hidden complex nature. The women easily convince Beatrice who, when left alone, 'realises' she also loves Benedick. This is the other half of the **gulling** scene.

The men then find Benedick and prod fun at him, saying he seems sad. Benedick admits that he is not himself and asks to speak to Leonato on his own, presumably to propose marriage. Don Jon arrives and tells Don Pedro and Claudio that Hero has been unfaithful and if they go to Hero's window, he can prove it. If it is true, Claudio will publicly shame Hero at their wedding.

Later, Borachio and Conrad are overheard bragging about their role in this scheme – Borachio had sex with Margaret in Hero's window (calling her "Hero") while Don Pedro and Claudio were able to see. Borachio and Conrad are overheard by some rather foolish, comic policemen – but they are arrested.

The next day Hero gets ready for her wedding, unaware of what will happen, and the policemen try to approach Leonato (as governor of the island) about their arrest from last night. Leonato is annoyed at the foolishness of the policemen and sends them away, telling them to conduct the interrogation.

Act 4

The wedding crowd gathers, and Claudio publicly denounces Hero for infidelity with Don Pedro claiming he witnessed it. The men then leave. Hero collapses and Leonato wishes she had never been born but Beatrice and the Friar conducting the marriage defend Hero. She then awakens and assures them she is innocent. The Friar forms a plan to pretend Hero has died from the shock. Everyone agrees to this plan and goes off, leaving Benedick and Beatrice on the stage alone. They finally confess their love, but Beatrice demands Benedick kill Claudio for her. He agrees.

Borachio and Conrad are interviewed by the Sexton (local magistrate) and their plan is revealed. The Sexton also mentions that Don Jon has run away in the night.

Act 5

Leonato and Antonio find Claudio and Don Pedro and challenge them to a duel. This is refused, and the older men leave. Then Benedick arrives and is mocked for being so serious looking. He informs them that Don Jon has fled, and he challenges Claudio to duel. He then leaves.

And then the Sexton arrives with his prisoners, Borachio and Conrad, and Don Jon's plan is revealed. Don Pedro and Claudio realise their mistake and Leonato arrives, accusing them of murdering Hero unfairly. To right the mistake, Claudio agrees to marry an unknown niece of Leonato's without seeing her.

The final scene has all the characters at a wedding. Hero is masked at the altar, pretending to be a niece of Leonato's. When Claudio goes to take her hand, she reveals her identity. Benedick also asks for permission to marry Beatrice at the same time, but Beatrice initially refuses. They realise they were tricked by their friends – but poems written for each other are revealed which prove they really love each other.

The play ends with two married couples and Don Pedro is told to find himself a wife. Don Jon is also captured off stage.

Main Themes

Yeah, but what is it all about?

A theme is an idea or message crafted by the writer (or rising out of the text) that engages the audience to think. It is an idea or message not just about the events or characters, but something wider – it is a philosophical, social, or moral point about the whole world or society.

It is often linked to the 'message' of the play or what the audience is supposed to 'learn from' the play. These aren't exactly what a theme are, but they are a good starting point to begin to wrap your head around what it is.

Ultimately, it is the 'point' of the play; the thing we, the viewer, are supposed to 'take' away from having watched it.

Themes are important parts of texts – but are difficult!

Understanding of theme is important if you are looking to enter those top bands and get those top grades. Thematic understanding – and theme-based essays – allow you to discuss the 'big ideas' of the text and, therefore, allow you to show how smart you are.

It is also usually in the mark scheme. What you have learned/taken away from the text (what has stuck with you) is usually part of the mark scheme. We can acknowledge this in the conclusion, sometimes as simple as "This drama has taught me that ..." and then we discuss a major theme **relevant to task**.

16

Theme 1: Deceit

Deception is an integral element of this play, yet it is not presented as a purely negative or positive trait. For example, deception allows Benedick and Beatrice to realise their love for each other, but it also allows Don Jon to trick Claudio into believing Hero has cheated on him. Instead, Shakespeare seems to present it is a social tool which can be used for good or bad. This 'dark' edge to the tool of deception serves as a warning from Shakespeare, but the positivity (especially its role in love and matching) cannot be dismissed either. Shakespeare presents a world where deception is part of the fabric and acknowledges the joy and pain that it can bring to us.

Theme 2: Social capital/standing

Social capital is the phrase used to decide the value of your place within the society you live. It is a combination of power, money, influence, and reputation. Social capital is influenced also by gender, intelligence, good looks, and family name. Social capital can rise and fall and, interestingly, can be affected by subjective gossip – how others view us or what they think of us can affect our social standing.

For example, Claudio places his reputation and need for a 'good' name above his love for Hero. The shame of a potential cheater as a wife is so much that, in fact, he publicly destroys her. Yet this is not true – Hero's social capital is completely destroyed by a mere rumour created by Don Jon. Notice how powerless Hero is to defend her place in society from this – her social capital is, in part, defined by the men around her.

This creates a highly **stratified** or controlling and layered society which constrains the ability of people to interact honestly. There are some who have more leeway (for example, Benedick and Beatrice) but they are still, ultimately, controlled by their place in society. Shakespeare seems to criticise this kind of society by showing its effect on innocent Hero.

Theme 3: Social graces

Much Ado About Nothing is a play set in a very controlled society. Men and women were expected to interact with very formal and flowery language, dominated by metaphor and almost-poetry like phrases. This **façade** of social grace and language creates inauthenticity inside the interactions between people. This is most obvious when the characters first meet. Leonato, due to social grace, is almost forced to invite Don Pedro and his soldiers to stay for a month (a huge and expensive undertaking) while Don Pedro is almost painfully polite about accepting the offer. There is nothing genuine in their interactions. This can also be seen in Claudio's attempts to speak to Hero which are described like a "banquet" of language.

Shakespeare is very much criticising this formal and stilted style of speech. This can be most clearly seen in the night's watch characters who try to speak in this style but fail miserably, creating word salad that means nothing. Shakespeare is setting this still of language up as laughable and silly.

Theme 4: Romantic love

Shakespeare presents romantic love as something public. Claudio and Hero's relationship is organised by Don Pedro and Leonato, and Benedick and Beatrice's relationship by the whole court, seemingly against their will at some parts. It is society that decides who should be matched rather than individuals.

Romantic love is also presented as having practical considerations. For example, Claudio checks if Hero is Leonato's heir before considering her a match. Her social standing and financial position are important factors. This is often criticised by a modern audience who see Benedick/Beatrice as 'more in love', but Shakespeare devotes as much time to Hero and Claudio. He doesn't seem to be criticising their match – but does presents Beatrice and Benedick as having more freedom due to their lack of social responsibility.

Theme 5: Masculinity and honour

This play, at first, seems to be about love and marriage as those themes are so obvious. The audience are also so often taken with Beatrice, a powerful female figure, that we forget that the majority of characters (and the most powerful) are men. Masculinity and male honour drive much of this play.

Don Pedro, Claudio, and Benedick are soldiers who have just been at war. Their relationship is founded on violence and trust in dangerous situations. Arriving in Messina is supposed to be almost a reward for their masculinity and service: this almost Eden-like environment where beautiful women are protected and there is plenty of food and wine. Don Pedro and Benedick, being more experienced, are able to make this transition from war to love much more smoothly than Claudio, who seems very uncomfortable and shy in this differing environment.

Male relationships play an important part in the narrative. Don Pedro's status means that, even if Claudio had wished to woo Hero on his own, he is almost unable to say no to Don Pedro due to their imbalanced relationship. This is also true of Leonato when he is approached by Don Pedro – could he really say no to the Prince when he asks for Claudio to marry Hero? In this situation, Hero can almost be viewed as a gift from Don Pedro to Claudio (along with Leonato's title and wealth) for his service in the war. Masculinity rewarding masculinity.

It is also a fear of losing his masculinity – and therefore his social standing as a soldier – that drives Claudio to publicly shame Hero. It is his masculinity that is threatened by becoming a **cuckold** and, so, this cannot be tolerated. Don Pedro supports this shaming to support his friend, yes, but also because Don Pedro's own masculine status is threatened – he vouched for Hero and he arranged the match between the two. And notice masculinity's answer to the problems of the play: duelling and violence! It is the Friar (a man outside of traditional masculine role) who manages to break that cycle just in time.

Shakespeare presents masculinity as powerful but fragile.

Theme 6: Wit

This was the ability of a person to control language both to express themselves and create a place within society. It is also a tool used to dominate and control others. This is most obviously seen in Beatrice and Benedick, who earn a lot of their social standing and power due to being 'wits'. In fact, their warring is a very public affair, almost like a sport to be watched and admired by others. This is often compared to warfare or jousting, with successful jibes compared to wounds.

Beatrice's intelligence and power as a wit gives her an acceptable place to both attack those in more powerful positions than her (such as Benedick and even Don Pedro) as well as the ability to reject social norms that are expected of women (like rejecting the idea of marriage). It even allows her to manipulate those around her to achieve her desired outcomes, such as revenge on Claudio through Benedick.

This strongly contrasts with those characters who do not have wit, for example Claudio. They seem dull and boring comparatively, and certainly makes them less memorable to the audience. They become almost background figures. Shakespeare seems to present wit (intelligence, linguistic power, imagination) as a heightened state of life and something enviable.

It is also interesting to note that Hero is presented as perfectly capable as a wit. In fact, in the tricking of Beatrice, Hero gets the better of her (apparently) more intelligent cousin. So, what prevents Hero from being seen as a wit? Well, she restrains herself because her societal role as 'daughter' and 'heir' to Leonato take precedence. Hero is forced to restrain herself to present as a 'good' and 'dutiful' (i.e. quiet and biddable) daughter. Beatrice does not have these social constraints.

And both Beatrice and Benedick in the end meet societal expectations of marriage and conform. Their wit is presented as a stumbling block to their love and, so, needs dismantled to allow them to be happy. Shakespeare seems to present wit as a state of existence, but not one that can be maintained for life.

Theme 7: Masquerade

Pretence and masks play a huge role within this play. They feature literally (the masque, the masks worn by the women at the end) but also in a more metaphorical sense (characters pretending to be what they are not, for example Don Jon, or being confused for others). Shakespeare is teaching a very basic lesson about not trusting appearances and what we see may not necessarily be a reflected truth.

But Shakespeare message could be considered more complex when we look at what occurs due to masks – Claudio and Hero express their love and a marriage is arranged, and Beatrice and Benedick are set up. Shakespeare presents masquerade as part of the 'game' of love – showing the best versions of ourselves, for example, to attract a partner.

Shakespeare is showing us that masks and pretence are potent forces in the game of love – but to be wary of them.

Theme 7: 'Noting' or noticing / seeing

In Shakespeare's time, the word "nothing" was pronounced very similarly to the word 'noting' which means to notice or take note of an event/person. This means that one reading of the title is *Much Ado About Noting/Seeing*, which is in fact the plot of the play: a series of events caused by seeing!

But be clear that much of the plot of this play revolves around mis-seeing or seeing improperly. For example, Claudio does a poor job of 'noting' Hero and accuses her of something that she did not do. The Friar at the end, in contrast, has clear sight and 'notes' Hero correctly as innocent. Beatrice and Benedick are also tricked into loving each other though false 'noting' of their friends, which is used to reveal a truth about themselves: that they are in love.

Shakespeare is showing us how imperfectly we see the world and those around us, how easily tricked we are.

Main quotations

Some of the big quotes and analysis

This is a play that is packed full of 'quotes' that you could learn and analyse. There is no real way – or real need – to cover every single quotation. I have chosen what, to me, seem the most important or the most generally useable in a critical response.

Since you are probably thinking of writing an essay, the quotes are arranged chronologically from beginning to end. This allows you to choose quotes from the beginning, middle and end of the play – exam boards usually wants to see this. Any good essay will have **coverage** of the whole text, not just one part.

Each quote is also labelled with what **tasks** it will be useful for, for example what themes it discusses or what character it reveals. This will allow you to start thinking not just about analysis of quotes, but also how they might be used in order to answer a question in essay format.

Much of the analysis you will find here is 'commonly accepted' (i.e. most people would agree that this is what these lines mean or why they were written) but there is always room for your own ideas or differing interpretations.

You may have studied one of these quotations in your classroom and your teacher may have taught you something different – even the opposite – but the beauty of Shakespeare lies in the complexity … there's room for multiple answers!

The title

Much Ado About Nothing

The phrase "Much Ado" means a lot of discussion or problems, yet the word "ado" has connotations of frivolous or unreal problems. "Much Ado" is very similar to the British phrase of 'a big fuss' or lots of bother over nothing. This sets the comedic and unreal tone very the beginning – the problems that are generated within this play are not real.

The word "nothing" has multiple meanings to be examined.

Firstly, "nothing" in the most obvious sense means the same as the above – that the problems that seem real in this play are not and that the characters are making a 'fuss'. This turns out to be literally true also since, for the most part, many of the problems are both made up and never cause anyone any real danger. They are "nothing" in the sense of not existing and "nothing" in the sense that they do not cause any real or lasting trouble.

Secondly, "nothing" in Shakespeare's time would have been pronounced identically to "noting". This is a word that means to see or understanding clearly. Therefore, the play title can be referred to as *Much Ado About Seeing*, which is exactly what happens in the play! People seeing each other causes "much ado" or a fuss – both in the sense that people literally see each other (like Benedick and Beatrice spying on others) or in the sense of seeing each other truly (i.e. Claudio is unable to 'note' Hero correctly and therefore causes problems).

Thirdly, "nothing" is a word related to absence and, so, becomes a pun or slang word for vagina or female genitalia (i.e. because they have "nothing" in their underwear basically). This means the title could mean *Much Ado About Women/The Vagina*. Once again, this is literally true within the play because Hero's virginity (or perceived lack of) is the source of many problems within the play. All of the male characters within the play spend a great deal of time focusing upon Hero's sexual history and her fitness to marry, causing "much ado".

Tasks: confusion; noting; women/sexuality/gender.

Act 1

*"I pray you, is Signior Mountanto
returned from the wars or no?"*

Beatrice, Act 1 Scene 1

Before Don Pedro and his soldiers arrive, they are discussed by Leonato and his family. Beatrice's very first line is a question about Benedick – which shows her interest in him.

She uses a metaphor to describe him: "mountanto". This is a movement in fencing which is seen as over-the-top and showing off. She is, therefore, call him 'Mr Show-off'. She is showing her disdain for him but tucked inside the question could be a genuine concern about whether or not he has survived ("returned from the wars or no?").

Tasks: Benedick; Beatrice; wit; love.

*"There is a kind of merry war
betwixt Signior Benedick and her"*

Leonato, Act 1 Scene 1

Beatrice thoroughly ridicules Benedick to the messenger and Leonato attempts to excuse his niece's seeming hostility. He uses the oxymoron of "merry war" to describe the interactions between Beatrice and Benedick.

The word "merry" encapsulates the humour in the war of wits for the onlookers, but also seems to imply that the two people themselves enjoy their arguments.

Yet the word "war" has implications of violence and destruction, showing that they have the true capability of hurting the other with their words.

The word "war" also has implications of a winner, which usually seems to be Beatrice as she is the faster and smarter of the two, but Benedick is a soldier and used to winning "war".

Tasks: Benedick; Beatrice; wit; love.

"Good Signior Leonato, you are come to meet your trouble: the fashion of the world is to avoid cost, and you encounter it."

Don Pedro, Act 1 Scene 1

The Prince and his men arrive. He and Leonato speak in overly courtly and polite language, showing the audience that the interactions in Messina will be controlled by courtly rules and social standing/graces are important.

Don Pedro also acknowledges the "cost" of having the soldiers to stay and the "trouble" it will cause. Yet Don Pedro does not mitigate it by offering money or attempt to lessen it by offering to stay less time – Leonato is one of his subjects after all.

Don Pedro is showing good grace but exercising power over Leonato. His social standing and power/honour are considerably above that of Leonato so Don Pedro can be polite but tucked inside them are commands to Leonato who cannot ignore them.

Tasks: masculinity; social standing; social graces.

"I wonder that you will still be talking, Signior Benedick: nobody marks you."

Beatrice, Act 1 Scene 1

Benedick makes a silly joke (that Leonato cannot be Hero's father as she is too pretty) and Beatrice immediately interjects. She is both defending her uncle, but also there is a sense of jealousy that she is not the centre of attention (Benedick is being the 'funny' one) and she has not been noticed by Benedick yet.

She says that no-one pays attention to him ("nobody marks you") implying that he is not worthy of attention or is just silly. This is a very forthright attack on his honour, which she is able to get away with due to the "merry war".

Yet, this is one of the first mentions of 'noting'. She is also saying that nobody sees him in the same way that she does – no-one realises that he is a fraud but that she does.

Tasks: Benedick; Beatrice; wit; noting.

"I had rather hear my dog bark at a crow, than a man swear he loves me."

Beatrice, Act 1 Scene 1

Beatrice immediately dismisses the idea of romantic love and, by extension, the idea of marriage. She states she would "rather hear" an annoying noise ("my dog bark at a crow") than a man proclaims his love for her. This is, of course, hyperbolic, and over-the-top. It is intended to make the crowd laugh, but it does express a truth that Beatrice believes about herself here: that she is better off without a man and doesn't need one. This is an unusual and independent statement to make, one that she gets away with as she is not Leonato's heir. Hero couldn't say this.

In this sentence she makes a comparison between "my dog" and "a man" – implying that men are animals and not in control of themselves, like the dog with the crow. It is also interesting she compares two noises: "bark/swear". Here she is implying that a man's proclamation of love is as meaningless and senseless as a dog's "bark" and is something reflexive and not to be trusted.

Tasks: Iago; class; jealousy.

"But keep your way, i' God's name; I have done."

Benedick, Act 1 Scene 1

Benedick gives one final insult and then puts a stop to the arguing ("I have done"). He puts her in her place, as it were, telling her to mind her manners ("keep your way"). It is a rather patronising line as he exercises masculine power over her. It implies that he cannot compete on her level of intelligence and 'wit' – that she is getting the better of him.

He feigns exhaustion ("done"), as if he can't go on because he is so tired, but really he knows he is losing the "battle" to her. Beatrice has reached the end of the line – she cannot push this much further without breaking the rules of propriety.

Tasks: Beatrice; Benedick; social standing; masculinity; wit.

"You always end with a jade's trick: I know you of old."

Beatrice, Act 1 Scene 1

Beatrice accuses him of dropping out of the argument like a horse out of a race: "a jade's trick" is when a poorly horse is made to look young and healthy but cannot last the full race. It is a reference to appearing one thing (smart, funny, witty, gentlemanly) but being another (poor, unable to keep up). It is, in a way, another 'noting' – she sees through him.

The phrase "I know you of old" is a pun: it references both previous arguments and how he has ended them before by exercising his masculine power; but is also a subtle hint at their romantic past and how he abandoned her before. It shows that she has not forgotten what he has done to her in the past.

Tasks: Beatrice; Benedick; wit; noting.

"In time the savage bull doth bear the yoke."

Don Pedro, Act 1 Scene 1

Don Pedro and Benedick argue about whether or not Benedick will ever marry. Benedick compares himself to a "bull" (i.e. animalistic and sexual) and implies that men should be with multiple women and not just one. Don Pedro then uses the above **aphorism** (common saying). The "yoke" is the instrument attached to cows and horses to turn them into domesticated farm animals. It is considered a way to trap but also to make them useful. Don Pedro is saying that even the most powerful men submit ("bear") to marriage to become members of society.

Yet this is still a very negative picture of marriage presented. Despite how much time is spent talking about it in this play, the men don't really seem to enjoy the idea of getting married – it is just what you 'do' and something that happens 'to' you. But this is how they speak only when amongst other men!

Bulls were also a symbol of the **cuckold** and, therefore, implies that all marriages involving cheating.

Tasks: Benedick; marriage; romantic love; society.

"Hath Leonato any son, my lord?"

Claudio, Act 1 Scene 1

Claudio checks with Don Pedro if Hero inherits Leonato's title and wealth before deciding to propose to her. This shows the practicality that underpins marriage at the time (it was as much about social standing as romantic love). Claudio tries to make the question seem casual, but it is very pointed and important to him – as would Claudio's social standing be to Hero.

Tasks: Romantic love; marriage; social standing.

"I cannot hide what I am: I must be sad when I have cause and smile at no man's jests"

Don Jon, Act 1 Scene 3

Conrad attempts to convince Don Jon to be nicer to his brother, Don Pedro, in order to gain his favour – especially as Don Jon led a revolt to try to kill his brother and take his throne. Don Jon rejects this idea saying he cannot "hide" that he is unhappy and miserable with his brother. He uses the modal verb of "must" to show the audience that he has no choice, that he cannot "hide" his nature. This puts him in stark contrast with the other characters, especially as they are about to enter the masque ball and pretending to be each other.

Don Jon seems surly, unhappy, and reticent to speak in contrast with all the others – but, in fact, Beatrice compliments him for his lack of talking, saying it is a positive. But in this situation his quietness is presented as natural and a sign of his bad nature.

Shakespeare sets up this contrast to emphasise Don Jon's difference, but it is also some rather lazy writing – Don Jon is not meant to be a complex and realistic villain. He does bad things because he "cannot hide" that he is bad and allows the plot to move along, adding complications to the narrative. Shakespeare makes him open about being a villain because it makes it easier to move the plot along.

Tasks: Don Jon; stage craft; manipulation; narrative.

"I had rather be a canker in a hedge

than a rose in his grace"

Don Jon, Act 1 Scene 3

Once again, Don Jon expresses his nature as a villain and his dislike of Don Pedro. He sets up the contrast of being a natural and real "canker" as opposed to a fake "rose" by pretending to be nice to his brother when he doesn't wish to be. He acknowledges that he would have "his grace" (i.e. Don Pedro's good opinion and financial and social gain from this) but that this is a price not worth being the fake "rose" that he is expected to be.

"Canker" is a noun with connotations of poison and disease. Thee quite clearly apply to Don Jon and his attempted affect on the world of Messina, although he is not very successful at it. While "rose" has connotations of beauty and value, but Don Jon seems to be saying that this beauty is an illusion, lie or transitory.

Don Jon inverts the negative "canker" to be a positive as it represents realism while the positive "rose" is a negative because it represents falsehood and lies. Don Jon is drawing a distinction between reality ("canker") and perception or illusion ("rose") and is setting up which world he would rather live in.

In this sense, Don Jon also contrasts himself with Claudio and Benedick, who flourish in Don Pedro's "grace", like "rose[s]". Don Jon here seems to be implying that they are only friends with Don Pedro for what they can achieve (i.e. Claudio wants Hero). Don Jon seems to imply that even though he is evil or a villain, he is at least an honest person unlike many others in this play. There is a sense of a principled stance to his wickedness.

It is interesting to note that Don Jon is one of the few characters who realises the unreality or illusionary world that they are currently living in when they arrive at Messina. The other characters seem to fall into the spell of this perfect place (often presented as a garden, like the Garden of Eden) but Don Jon refuses the illusion, even if it would bring him closer to money and power again. Don Jon chooses reality/darkness.

Tasks: Don Jon; illusion versus reality.

Act 2

"one is too like an image and says nothing, and the other too like my lady's eldest son, evermore tattling."

Beatrice, Act 2 Scene 1

Beatrice describes her perfect man as a combination of Benedick ("evermore tattling") and of Don Jon ("says nothing"). Beatrice lists a number of other qualities (making the picture of a man impossible to exist) but she puts 'wit' and talk at the top of her list, showing how important it is in the world of the play.

She sets these two characters in opposition and, therefore, implies the goodness of Benedick by opposing him to Don Jon. She implies that (at least in the world of the play!) communication skills are a sign of a good nature/good person.

Shakespeare also pokes fun at his own lazy writing through Beatrice, calling Don Jon more an "image" than a true character (i.e. flat and one dimensional).

Tasks: Beatrice; Benedick; Don Jon; wit/communication.

"away to Saint Peter for the heavens; he shows me where the bachelors sit, and there live we as merry as the day is long."

Beatrice, Act 2 Scene 1

Beatrice describes dying without marrying and that, because she would still be a virgin, she would immediately go to heaven (notice Shakespeare asserts Beatrice's virginity as a sign of her goodness). Beatrice does not assert herself as an old 'maid' but rather compares herself to a "bachelor".

Beatrice is asserting her own masculine, non-feminine social position because an 'old maid' would be considered a negative, but a "bachelor" is not, which is what she sees herself as. She is also gently poking fun at the double standard which allows men not to marry (remaining "bachelors") but which puts pressure upon her to marry and find a husband when she doesn't wish to.

Tasks: Beatrice; marriage; gender.

"Daughter, remember what I told you: if the prince

do solicit you in that kind, you know your answer."

Leonato, Act 2 Scene 1

Following Beatrice's ridicule of marriage and refusal to marry (even if only a joke), Leonato instructs Hero that she must accept Don Pedro if he asks ("you know your answer").

He is asserting his masculine and fatherly control over his daughter, who has no choice in this situation ("what I told you").

The use of pronouns and word order are interesting as Leonato puts himself ("I") at the start of the sentence and Hero and her wishes ("you") towards the end. He also asserts that, despite it being his instruction, it is her ("your") answer and not his. He asserts power and demands she take his will as if it were her own – this is very possessive and controlling.

Tasks: Leonato; Hero; masculinity; marriage; social grace.

"he is the prince's jester: a very dull fool"

Beatrice, Act 2 Scene 1

Beatrice and Benedick have an insulting conversation about each other while Benedick is in a mask pretending not to be himself. Depending on the staging, Beatrice either doesn't know and accidentally insults him ("fool") or she knows and is deliberately goading him, using the situation because he can't talk back.

The word "dull" has connotations of stupid and boring, while "jester" implies a clown and lacking in substance. The possessive "prince's" also implies that he is not his own man, has little independence, and is a 'hanger-on' of more powerful men. Beatrice insults what Benedick takes personal pride in (his wit and intelligence) and professional pride (being a soldier).

Benedick holds on to these grudges for a chunk of the play. It is possible he had the mask on and was talking to her in the hopes of hearing something positive as he already knew he was in love.

Tasks: Beatrice; Benedick; masks; romantic love.

"Thus answer I in the name of Benedick,

But hear these ill news with the ears of Claudio."

Claudio, Act 2 Scene 1

Claudio is convinced by Don Jon that Don Pedro woos Hero for himself. Claudio shows his gullibility to the audience by believing it, a feature which is established due to its importance for later. It shows Claudio's youth and trusting nature, but also his naivety and his lack of experience in the arenas of love.

Notice that Claudio breaks down the various elements of identity (seen in the name use of "Benedick/Claudio") into smaller parts ("name/ears"). This implies that identity for Claudio is a fractured thing, something that we put on and wear like a mask. Identity is just a name that we put on and is made up of small bits we put on also. This is also represented by how quickly he changes his name to pretend to be Benedick.

Claudio doesn't really know who he is and lacks a stable inner nature, which contrasts with Benedick and Beatrice who are so overpoweringly 'themselves' that, in fact, their stubbornness stands in the way of their own happiness to some extent.

This is a theme which persists for Claudio and, to some extent, Hero. The idea that they don't have a single identity or personality but, in fact, change depending on the situation that they find themselves. The pressures of society and the people they meet change them from scene to scene. In fact, Claudio goes from solider to lover to villain for example for very flimsy reasons and excuse.

This could be Shakespeare making a point about young people and how they don't 'know' themselves well yet, or this could just be a plot device that allow Shakespeare to make Claudio change so extremely throughout the play depending on the situation in order to make the narrative make sense.

Or it could be both – this is Shakespeare after all!

Tasks: Claudio; identity; masks; romantic love; deceit.

"she speaks poniards, and every word stabs"
Benedick, Act 2 Scene 1

Don Pedro tells Benedick that Beatrice is angry with him, and Benedick loses his temper. He uses this metaphor to describe how powerful her wit is and how much it hurts him. He compares her language to "poniards", which are small knives that cause small but intense cuts. Her "words" are war-like that "stab" and cause injury and pain. Benedick uses the language to war to express both their relationship and that he feels like a casualty, a wounded and attacked party. It also shows how powerful she is and how over-matched he is. He is losing.

Tasks: Benedick; Beatrice; wit.

"he lent it me awhile; and I gave him use for it,
a double heart for his single one:
marry, once before he won it of me with false dice"
Beatrice, Act 2 Scene 1

Don Pedro tells Beatrice she has "lost the heart" of Benedick and she responds by telling him about their romantic past. She uses the extended metaphor of physically giving a "heart" to represent love and romance. He initially proclaimed to love her ("he lent it me") and she returned that love ("a double heart") but he lied to her about his intentions ("false dice").

The physical giving of a "heart" is common romantic love poetry imagery. Beatrice starts by using this to show that her love was initially honest. She then perverts this imagery by using the language of games ("won/false dice") to show that Benedick had been playing with her and she hadn't known.

Interestingly, their initially romantic interest as a game semi-continues throughout the play: their arguing is often linked to a kind of game or "merry war". This implies that their romantic relationship didn't end (the game never stopped) but it changed into something else – this arguing which they do now.

Tasks: Benedick; Beatrice; romantic love; wit.

"Here, Claudio, I have wooed in thy name,

and fair Hero is won"

Don Pedro, Act 2 Scene 1

Don Jon's plan collapses very quickly, and Don Pedro has been true to his word. The use of deceit and masks ("wooed in thy name") has been successful. It is set up as a game that is "won", implying once again that love is a game to be played.

It is interesting that the game is played more successfully in this play when others intervene. Hero and Claudio's marriage is arranged very quickly, whilst Benedick and Beatrice have been in an on-off again relationship for a long time because they have no 'help' yet from the wider society of Messina.

Hero is also "won" like an object, showing her place and social position as daughter and heir in Messina.

Tasks: Romantic love; social position; masculinity; gender.

"No, my lord, unless I might have another for working-days: your grace is too costly to wear every day"

Beatrice, Act 2 Scene 1

Don Pedro proposes marriage to Beatrice. It is almost always presented as a 'joke' from Don Pedro by directors, but it is possible the Prince is showing a romantic interest in Beatrice. You could see the above sentence as him 'testing the waters'. She is described as beautiful and he mentions on a number of occasions that he finds her funny and charming.

Beatrice rejects him ("No, my lord"). She is still respectful ("my lord") and plays up his masculinity and her weakened social status ("lord") to soften the blow. She also uses humour ("your grace is too costly") to further soften the rejection. She uses her wit in order to avoid marriage, even with this powerful man.

The audience begin to suspect that she and Benedick are, in fact, destined to be together.

Tasks: Beatrice; wit; marriage; masculinity.

"his words are a very fantastical banquet"
Benedick, Act 2 Scene 3

Benedick delivers a **soliloquy** (a speech to the audience) about the change in Claudio since he has fallen in love with Hero. Claudio is no longer a soldier but is now more a poet ("his words are a very fantastical"). Benedick focuses on the change of Claudio's language as language and wit are such important features within this play. Benedick ridicules the language of love, comparing it to food. He describes Claudio as a glutton (a greedy person) who cannot control himself ("just so many"). The words "fantastical" imply that Claudio has become silly and over-the-top. This entire speech is ironic because the minute Benedick admits his love for Beatrice, he begins to write bad love poetry!

Tasks: Benedick; romantic love; communication.

"she loves him with an enraged affection"
Leonato, Act 2 Scene 3

This is the **gulling** of Benedick scene. Leonato pretends that Beatrice "loves" Benedick, loud enough for him to overhear. This is both a narrative (moves the plot along) and comic moment – the men (Leonato, Don Pedro, etc) are meant to be speaking so loudly and slowly to be heard that is obvious they are tricking Benedick. But Benedick is so desperate to hear this (because it is secretly what he wants to hear) he ignores how obvious the trick is. He wants to be gulled; he wants to be tricked.

Leonato intertwines the idea of passion ("loves/affection") with anger ("enraged"). This is how they build up the idea of Beatrice hiding her love for Benedick behind her anger then whenever she shouts him it is because she loves him and is frustrated not to have him ("past the infinite of thought"). Benedick takes this to mean that Beatrice's disdain and dislike are a sign of her love.

Tasks: Romantic love; deceit; Beatrice; Benedick.

"By this day! she's a fair lady:

I do spy some marks of love in her."

Benedick, Act 2 Scene 3

After being 'gulled', Benedick is on stage alone and very quickly changes his mind about Beatrice. He appreciates her beauty ("she's a fair lady") but also acknowledges that she is smart and funny. It is possible that he has just fallen in love with her, but it seems more likely that the 'gulling' is more Benedick's chance to admit that he has always secretly been in love with Beatrice and that they are a perfect match for each other.

The men have sent Beatrice out to call Benedick in for dinner and he believes that her angry expression is proof of her love that she is trying to cover up ("spy some marks of love"). This is one of many examples of **inversion**: where things mean their opposites or look their opposites. In this case, Benedick thinks that Beatrice's open hostility and dislike in her facial expression indicates the depth of her love for him. It is also another example of looking, noticing and seeing – in this case, seeing wrongly!

Tasks: Deceit; gulling; romantic love; Benedick; noticing

"Ha! 'Against my will I am sent to bid you come in

to dinner;' there's a double meaning in that"

Benedick, Act 2 Scene 3

Beatrice makes it clear to Benedick that, at this stage, she doesn't like him ("against my will") but, as the other characters had anticipated, Benedick hears something in the sentence ("a double meaning") that proves she loves him. There is no "double meaning" that can be found – it is crystal clear – but it shows the power of self-delusion and the subjective nature of the world that he hears something that is not there.

A similar bias happens to Claudio when his distrust of women/Hero is reinforced by seemingly innocent events – but to more negative effects. There is a lesson here about trust!

Tasks: Deceit; gulling; romantic love; Benedick.

Act 3

"Nature never framed a woman's heart
Of prouder stuff than that of Beatrice;
Disdain and scorn ride sparkling in her eyes"
Hero, Act 3, Scene 1

Hero and Ursula gull Beatrice as she follows them secretly in the garden. Hero, a normally reserved character due to her social place as Leonato's daughter and heir, is more communicative and intelligent than she appears in much of the play. In this all-female space, Hero is in charge and as 'witty' as her cousin.

Hero employs hyperbole and exaggeration ("never framed a woman's heart of prouder stuff") and a metaphor ("disdain and scorn ride sparkling in her eyes") to create a sense of imagery and power to tricking of Beatrice, showing her intelligence.

The strength of the word choice on "sparkling" indicates not only Beatrice's depth of faults (pride, "disdain and scorn") but also her enjoyment and these faults. They imply that Beatrice is self-delusional, unable to see herself correctly. Hero takes Beatrice's greatest assets (intelligence and independence) and that they stand in the way of true seeing and happiness with Benedick.

Tasks: Hero; Beatrice; gulling; deceit; romantic love

"What fire is in mine ears? Can this be true?
Stand I condemn'd for pride and scorn so much?
Contempt, farewell! and maiden pride, adieu!"
Beatrice, Act 3, Scene 1

Beatrice's use of questions shows her confusion at the situation and disbelief, while her use of exclamation marks indicates the strength of her newfound love for Benedick. The shortness of the sentences ironically reflects how quickly Beatrice's opinion of Benedick changes, how short a time it takes for her to love him.

Tasks: Beatrice; gulling; deceit; romantic love

"his jesting spirit; which is now crept into a lute-string"

Claudio, Act 3, Scene 2

Claudio and Don Pedro make fun of the change in Benedick, that he no longer has a "jesting spirit". He has stopped being so aggressive in his 'wit' and making comments against love. In fact, Benedick tries to cover it up as just toothache making him look so unhappy about the situation.

Instead Benedick has "crept into a lute-string", meaning that he has started to sigh a lot and write/sing love poems/songs for Beatrice. The other men notice this change and mock him for it, almost revelling in his change and fall from the bachelor he was.

Tasks: Benedick; masculinity; romantic love; deceit.

"the lady is disloyal"

Don Jon, Act 3, Scene 2

Don Jon begins his 'plan' to get in between Claudio and Hero by making Claudio think she has been "disloyal" (i.e. cheating and sexually active outside of marriage). These are huge accusations which affect Hero's standing within the community, and also hurt Claudio's masculine standing/pride to be attached to such a woman. Don Jon's deceit is not subtle, but it is effective.

Tasks: masculinity; deceit; social standing.

"If I see any thing to-night why I should not marry her to-morrow in the congregation, where I should wed, there will I shame her."

Claudio, Act 3, Scene 2

Despite using the "If" statement, which implies doubt, it seems here that Claudio has almost made up his mind that he will "see any thing to-night". He also immediately decides on a course of action ("there will I shame her") which is public and cruel. It makes him seem naïve, easily manipulated, and childish.

Tasks: masculinity; deceit; social standing.

"the prince, Claudio and my master, planted and placed and possessed by my master Don John, saw afar off in the orchard this amiable encounter."

Borachio, Act 3, Scene 3

Borachio drunkenly relates what Don Jon has paid him to do: have sex with Margaret ("this amiable encounter") at Hero's window to make Don Pedro and Claudio think it was Hero. Borachio's language (the repetition of the p-sound and over-use of "and") reflect his drunken state. It is supposed to be the dead of night so Borachio is unaware he is being over-heard by the night watch (police/guards) – this is a negative inversion of the previous gulling scenes. This time hiding, noting and gossip are used to uncover an 'evil' plot against love instead of creating it.

Borachio also uses word choice to show the extent of Don Jon's scheme: "planted and placed and possessed". Don Jon's control of the situation (and therefore Claudio) is almost like demonic possession or control of an object.

Tasks: manipulation; deceit; masculinity; noting.

"We charge you, in the prince's name, stand!"

First Watchman, Act 3, Scene 3

Don Jon's plan collapses very quickly. Borachio and Conrad are taken into custody immediately. This sets up the eventual resolve of the play (the watchmen brining the evidence to Leonato) from the outset.

The phrase "charge you" shows the criminality of this deception and it is interesting to note the men exercise the "prince's name" in this situation. It is Don Pedro's de-facto power and role as monarch which is being exercised in this situation. Don Pedro's power is both the cause (his willingness to be led by his brother) but also the resolution of the situation.

The watchmen are presented as comic figures - but bring resolution to the negativity that overhangs this play.

Tasks: deceit; gulling; noting; manipulation; power.

"I am out of all other tune, methinks."

Beatrice, Act 3, Scene 4

The women arrive to prepare Hero for her wedding and Beatrice arrives looking unusual and not herself – a state described as being in a "sick tune". Beatrice uses her 'wit' to turn this into a rather sad pun about being out-of-tune or not usual self. Being in love affects both Benedick and Beatrice rather similarly – it affects their ability to be witty and funny. It takes away the edge and hardiness to their jibes.

Interestingly, Beatrice frames her love (and lack of wit) as being "out of all other tune" – like she is unable to play an instrument or being out of "tune" with herself. The love between her and Benedick is discordant and lacks rhythm and purpose, unlike the witty banter between them which is dominated by rhythm, rhyme, and interplay, much like music.

Beatrice is describing a lack of harmony in society, which is about to be expressed by Claudio's treatment of Hero.

Tasks: Beatrice; romantic love; wit; societal norms.

"Take their examination yourself and bring it me"

Leonato, Act 3, Scene 5

The watchmen come to Leonato to bring evidence of Borachio and Conrad's villainy and, therefore, Don Jon's. The watchmen are comic figures to try to speak like 'high born' men but muddle up the language to the extent that they speak in riddles or what sounds like nonsense. This irritates Leonato who calls them "tedious" (which the think is a compliment!).

Yet they hold the key to the happy ending of the play and Leonato fails to notice or see them properly – or to understand how important their visit is – and he sends them away ("take their examination yourself"). This failure to see what is important or necessary in any given moment is one of the reasons that Don Jon's plan is successful for so long.

Tasks: deceit; noting; wit; Leonato; manipulation.

Act 4

"Give not this rotten orange to your friend;

She's but the sign and semblance of her honour."

Claudio, Act 4, Scene 1

On the altar – and in front of the assembled community of Messina – Claudio openly mocks/rejects Hero as a wife. He calls her a "rotten orange". This implies that she is an object to be owned and thrown away ("orange") but has connotations of being spoiled ("rotten") due to her apparent sexual infidelity.

Notice that Claudio puts the male-male relationship between himself and Leonato ("your friend") above that of Leonato's with his own daughter. The idea in this sentence is that the masculine world of Messina is dominated by peer-to-peer relationships and that Hero's position is lesser, even if she is Leonato's family.

Claudio is once again shown to be someone with 'poor' sight. He confuses Don Jon's lies with truth which causes him to see Hero's "honour" as a lie ("sign and semblance") rather than the truth. This is a sign of Claudio's naivety but also a possible sign of his misogyny (he believes these lies about Hero very quickly). It is also a sign of Claudio's reputation being reliant upon his masculinity: he is terrified of being humiliated by Hero.

Tasks: Claudio; deceit; romantic love; gulling; noting.

"Sir, they are spoken, and these things are true."

Don Pedro, Act 4, Scene 1

There is an appeal to authority – both Leonato and Claudio look to Don Pedro to confirm or deny the charges against Hero. Don Pedro's language is respectful of Leonato ("sir") but calm and straightforward ("these things are true"). His authority as a Prince is called upon but is also dramatically ironic as the audience are aware that he is deceived. It is a false authority.

Tasks: authority; masculinity; deceit; social norms.

"But fare thee well, most foul, most fair! farewell,

Thou pure impiety and impious purity!"

Claudio, Act 4, Scene 1

Claudio speaks in a series of oxymorons, contrasting words/phrases that seem to contradict each other. This shows his confusion and the contrast/duality of Hero: the appearance of her as good contrasting with her 'secret' liaisons with men. This inside/outside divide is seen in the contrasting statements: "foul/impiety" referring to her apparent actions while "fair/pure" refer to her beauty and her reputation to the world. But Claudio is 'mis-seeing' the lady, caused by Don Jon.

These statements refer to other plays by Shakespeare. Romeo in *Romeo and Juliet* speaks in similar oxymorons to capture his confusion about love (how something 'good' can cause pain), while oxymorons in *Macbeth* show confusion about the good/bad of the witches who cause chaos. In fact, "foul/fair" are exactly the terms used in *Macbeth* to describe the destructive power of the witches.

Tasks: Claudio; romantic love; deceit; noting and seeing.

"Death is the fairest cover for her shame

That may be wish'd for."

Leonato, Act 4, Scene 1

Don Pedro and Claudio leave while Hero swoons, unable to stand the charges being levelled against her. The initial exclamation is that Hero has died of shock as Claudio's accusations could ruin her reputation and her social standing, bringing shame and social ruin on both herself and her father.

She has only fainted but, interestingly, Leonato claims that "death is the fairest cover for her shame". This implies that Leonato, in this moment, would rather have a dead daughter than one who has been disgraced. In this moment, he seems to believe the accusations although he later changes his mind.

Tasks: marriage; social norms; femininity; deceit.

"O, she is fallen into a pit of ink, that the wide sea

Hath drops too few to wash her clean"

Leonato, Act 4, Scene 1

Hero only fainted, and Leonato exclaims regret that she didn't die. His reaction to her shame is extreme and immediate. He compares her to a "fallen" angel – a devil. This implies that before this moment was a kind of Heaven which the accusation has destroyed and ruined for everyone. Shame is metaphorically compared to a "pit of ink", staining Hero who can never been "clean" again not even the "wide sea". Notice that there is no evidence (only the word of the men) and yet this claim is like "ink" that will forever stain the reputation of Hero. There is an implication of blackness and permanence to this insult.

Tasks: Leonato; fatherhood; shame; social norms.

"O, on my soul, my cousin is belied!"

Beatrice, Act 4, Scene 1

Beatrice defends her cousin instantly. Her strength of feeling can be seen in the sentence structure beginning with the "O" and ending in an exclamation mark. The depth of her feeling and trust can be seen in her language ("on my soul"), showing her certainty. Beatrice can 'see' correctly and may not be able to understand exactly what happened but knows it is wrong.

It is interesting that Beatrice describes Hero as "belied". The construction of this verb makes the lie seem like an assault or violence with the suffix of be- meaning 'around, from all sides'. This creates an image of Hero as being surrounded by lies, and Beatrice immediately 'sees' the violence being perpetrated.

Beatrice's strong defence of her cousin – and her rejection of the men's claims against her – show her unusual status within Leonato's household. Hero barely defends herself, but Beatrice shows many masculine qualities within her defence. She is rejecting the idea of being a meek and quiet woman.

Tasks: Beatrice; noting; deceit; social norms; femininity.

"Come, lady, die to live: this wedding-day

Perhaps is but prolong'd: have patience and endure."

Friar, Act 4, Scene 1

The priest creates a plan in which Hero will pretend to "die" to give Claudio time to calm down and realise his error! The oxymoron of "die to live" almost acknowledges how complicated the plan is. There is a sense here that Shakespeare is moving away from 'realism' and what would really happen into 'high drama' in order to create a neat resolution to the play.

The friar also gives a nod to the audience, almost breaking the fourth wall, that the happy ending is still to come; "this wedding-day perhaps is but prolong'd". The audience are being told that the marriage of Hero and Claudio will take place if we just 'hang in there' to the resolution of events. The friar is speaking to Hero but also the audience to "have patience and endure".

There is also an interesting idea contained within "die to live" which is that Hero must go through a death or transformation to rid herself of the metaphorical stain ("ink") and sin of Claudio's accusation. She may be innocence of charges, but she still must appear to suffer and "die" in order to be cleansed of these false charges, in order to regain her reputation. This is a sign of the weakness and instability of a woman's status and reputation, and the power and the authority of men, that a woman can have her status ruined by an unsubstantiated and untrue accusation without any evidence.

The plan that is put in place by the priest is reminiscent of Juliet's plan with the friar in *Romeo and Juliet*, which is to fake death in order to buy time and change a man's opinion. In Juliet's case it was the opinion of her father, but the similarity still stands. There is a sense of the use of 'death' as a tool to restore a woman's status and role. One could argue that Juliet represents the tragic outcome of such a deception and plan, while Hero is the other side of the same coin – a happier outcome where events go as they are supposed to.

Tasks: marriage; deceit; societal norms; femininity.

"I do love nothing in the world so well as you:

Is not that strange?"

Benedick, Act 4, Scene 1

After Hero's humiliation, all but Beatrice and Benedick leave the stage. This is the moment they finally confess their admiration and "love" for each other – although Benedick says it first, perhaps conforming to his role as the man. The language they use is simplistic and straightforward ("love nothing in the world so well as you") which contrasts with the puns and 'wit' used elsewhere. This shows the depth and sincerity of the emotions.

Benedick also expresses the volume and depth of his love by comparing it to "the world" in terms of size. This also implies that Beatrice is his world, his everything.

His use of a question and the word "strange" also imply his continuing amazement and confusion over these newfound feelings, showing his surprise at admitting them to her.

Tasks: Benedick; romantic love; social norms.

"Kill Claudio."

Beatrice, Act 4, Scene 1

Beatrice admits to loving Benedick back but, due to their history and his past flirtations, she shows reticence and disbelief. He says that he will prove it to her – she just needs to ask something of him, and he will do.

She responds with the short command "Kill Claudio". It is short, straightforward, and almost emotionless. It has no ability to be argued with or changed, which is very different from most of the language used between these characters. It is unarguable.

The word "kill" is aggressive, destructive, and angry. This shows the depth of Beatrice's fierce loyalty to her cousin, but also her sense of right and wrong as well as justice. It also shows her manipulative control and power over Benedick that he agrees.

Tasks: Beatrice; romantic love; revenge.

"O God, that I were a man! I would eat his heart

in the market-place."

Beatrice, Act 4, Scene 1

Beatrice expresses her anger and frustration at having to work through Benedick to have her revenge on Claudio. She expresses clearly that her emotions, desires, and power do not match her societal status due to her body as a woman.

Her exclamation ("O God") as well as her use of the exclamation mark show the strength of these feelings. She is almost calling out to God, as if she wished to be transformed or changed in order to have the violent powers that she so desires. There is also a sense of envy of Benedick, a jealous towards the freedoms that he has access to just from his gender.

Interestingly Beatrice expresses her anger as hyper-violent and hyper-masculine ("I would eat his heart"). She would utterly destroy him, beyond even the duel that Benedick is going to challenge him to. Beatrice seems to imply that she if "were a man", she would outstrip both Benedick and the others at their 'own game' as it were. She also describes how she would use this power freely and publicly ("in the market place"). She would have no fear or desire to hide from retribution.

Yet the description she outlines ("eat his heart") is animalistic and out of control. There is a sense in which she equates masculinity to a lack of control and an animal, base set of instincts. Beatrice sees femininity as being controlled or tamed, the counterbalance to masculinity which is not.

Beatrice feels like a wild animal who is 'trapped' in her gender.

A final note here is that Beatrice is also referencing the madness of the **sparagmos**. This is a religious rite where women (called Maenads) would gather to pull apart and then eat animals or men as a religious offering. This was part of Ancient Greek literature (with no indication it really happened) and was a sign of 'the madness of women' and their destructive power. Beatrice wishes to have this power but feels constrained.

Tasks: Beatrice; femininity; social norms; power.

"But manhood is melted into courtesies, valour into compliment, and men are only turned into tongue"

Beatrice, Act 4, Scene 1

Beatrice tries to provoke Benedick into killing his friend by insulting his masculinity ("manhood"). She uses a pun on both his character as well as his penis ("manhood") to imply that he has gone 'soft' ("melted") because he is not a 'real' man either in his character or his ability to maintain an erection.

She also uses a rule of three in a list to repeat this idea ("manhood/valour/men") more than once. She attacks all of the things that Benedick values as a soldier in this list.

She then finishes by insulting Benedick on what is one of his greatest strengths: his wit and power with language. She says that he is "turned into tongue", implying that he is all talk and not a real man of action or violence. The element of Benedick's character which he most values and is valued by others in this play (his "tongue") is mocked by her as not enough.

Interestingly Beatrice says this just after professing her love and hearing his – she is manipulating by implying that he won't be enough of a man for her with the only way to prove it is to kill her enemy (i.e. Claudio) who is Benedick's best friend.

Tasks: Beatrice; romantic love; revenge; language.

"Enough, I am engaged; I will challenge him"

Benedick, Act 4, Scene 1

Benedick is manipulated into undertaking what Beatrice desires – challenging Claudio to a duel. Benedick's sense of exhaustion and commitment can be seen in his plain word choice ("enough"). His commitment to her can be seen in the tense use ("I will"). Finally, her ironically uses the language of marriage ("I am engaged") layered with violence ("challenge") to show his love to her. Gone is the funny and happy character at the start. He now appears terse and unhappy: a soldier ready to fight.

Tasks: Benedick; masculinity; manipulation; power.

"Prince John is this morning secretly stolen away;

Hero was in this manner accused, in this very manner

refused, and upon the grief of this suddenly died."

Sexton, Act 4, Scene 2

The Sexton is a learned Church man brought in to transcribe the interrogation of Borachio and Conrad. As the men of the night's watch blunder around, he keeps the questioning rationale and on track. It is his cool head that unravels Don Jon's plan from Act 4 Scene 1 (the denouncing of hero) to Act 4 Scene 2 where the legal profession now has the evidence to exonerate Hero. The Sexton will take this evidence to Leonato's and begin to wrap up this play. Clear noting and seeing allows this.

It is the Sexton's clear seeing and mind that allow this play to avoid being a tragedy (the humiliation of Hero) and allows it to start to become a comedy (the marriage of Hero).

The Sexton also provides some extra context for the audience. We find out that Don Jon has run away ("secretly stolen away") presumably as he was expecting to be found out. The word "secretly" tells the audience how he left but is also ironically presented as it seems that everyone knows he has "stolen away". It is not much of a secret! The phrase "stolen away" is also interesting as it has an underhand and illicit, showing society's awareness that Don Jon has done something wrong although no one is yet aware of his role in Hero's humiliation. It is also ironic in that Don Jon has "stolen away" something – the good name and reputation of Hero and those he manipulated.

We also find out that the Sicilian society has 'bought' the lie that Hero has "suddenly died", a key element of the Friar's plan. It is the "grief" from these events that allow Leonato and Beatrice to control and manipulate Claudio and Don Pedro in the next Act. This grief at the supposed death of Hero allow them to set up the final gulling of the play – the manipulation of Claudio into marrying Hero. This grief for Hero also washes away any potential staining and sting that is left on her reputation.

Tasks: Don Jon; deceit; manipulation; noting.

Act 5

"[Hero] lies buried with her ancestors; O, in a tomb where never scandal slept, save this of hers, framed by thy villany!"

Leonato, Act 5, Scene 1

Leonato has worked himself up into a rage and encounters Claudio and Don Pedro. His opinion has changed wildly since Act 4 and now full believes that his daughter has been "framed" and that Claudio is responsible ("thy villany!"). The exclamation mark coupled with the very pointed pronoun ("thy") show the depth of his anger at the situation.

It is interesting to note that Leonato's anger is not just for his daughter, but also for his own reputation and his family name ("where scandal never slept"). Leonato's anger stems not just from the apparent death of his daughter ("lies buried") but also from Claudio and Don Pedro's general destruction of his masculinity and his family's reputation in Messina.

In fact, Leonato is so angered that he challenges Claudio to a duel – initially Claudio and Don Pedro laugh at him due to his age, which only further angers Leonato. Yet Leonato feels that he is defending not only his daughter but also himself and his reputation from this attack.

Tasks: masculinity; deceit; reputation; social norms.

"Art thou sick, or angry?"

Don Pedro, Act 5, Scene 1

Benedick arrives, meeting Claudio and Don Pedro just after Leonato leaves. They ask him to cheer them up, but he refuses. Don Pedro is confused by his disposition, as can be seen from the use of the question structure above.

The use of "sick" first and then "angry" shows his attempt to work out the situation and his inability to truly see/note Benedick. He is not able to 'read' the situation accurately.

Tasks: Benedick; romantic love; noting; masculinity.

"You are a villain; I jest not: I will make it good how you dare, with what you dare, and when you dare"

Benedick, Act 5, Scene 1

Benedick keeps his promise to Beatrice and challenges Claudio to a duel ("I will make it good"). Note the word choice here: "make it good" implies that this duel, this violence, will correct the violent done to Hero (and Beatrice). There is a sense in which strength is more important in resolving this situation than the 'wit' and mental agility prized earlier.

Benedick's direct address of Claudio ("you") and his word choice ("villain") are meant to provoke and anger Claudio, while showing him how serious Benedick is. This is further done in the repetition of "dare" in a rule of three, which is meant to imply that Claudio is a coward who is afraid. This is a direct attack on his masculinity to provoke him.

The broken sentence structure (the use of semi-colon and listing) reflects Benedick's broken and angry emotions. He feels torn between Beatrice and Claudio, showing in the torn sentence structure and its broken nature.

Tasks: Benedick; masculinity; romantic love; anger.

"My lord, for your many courtesies I thank you: I must discontinue your company: your brother the bastard is fled from Messina: you have among you killed a sweet and innocent lady."

Benedick, Act 5, Scene 1

Benedick goes one further than his promised duel: he breaks his friendship with Don Pedro ("I must discontinue your company"). This is a powerful friendship that Benedick gives up for love. His reasoning clear in the word choice surrounding Hero ("sweet and innocent lady") and his accusation ("you killed").

Interestingly, Benedick shows clear sight about Don Jon's role ("is fled from Messina") in a way that Don Pedro does not.

Tasks: Benedick; noting; masculinity; reputation.

"Don John your brother incensed me
to slander the Lady Hero"
Borachio, Act 5, Scene 1

The plot of Don Jon is revealed to Claudio and Don Pedro, and the power and narrative weight of this play as a tragedy collapses. There is a brief period where it seems that it could all go wrong, ending in even more death and destruction. But the intervention of the police (as silly as they appear) allows a route out of this tragedy and back to the comedy it started as.

The tension of the potential duels dissipates at this revelation and Hero's innocence is sealed ("slander") without a doubt. They both finally see the situation clearly now (it has been spelled out for them!). The next steps of Claudio and Don Pedro can now result in a positive ending – if they can calm down Benedick!

Tasks: tragedy; comedy; masculinity; noting.

"yet sinn'd I not but in mistaking"
Claudio, Act 5, Scene 1

Claudio and Don Pedro both apologise to Leonato for their role in the 'death' of Hero and offer penance – but they do it with the caveat that they didn't really know that they were doing anything wrong. They claim it was an honest mistake.

Notice that Claudio frames his crime has "sinn'd I not" – the evil or the deliberate violence towards Hero was not his fault. It wasn't a "sin" that he committed. Claudio does not acknowledge the cruel and public way he humiliated Hero and, instead, uses the situation as a form of absolution from his role in events.

Claudio positions his humiliation and 'murder' of Hero as a result of "mistaking" – misunderstanding, mis-seeing, and a mistake. All of these remove guilt and blame from him, instead making the situation seem like an accident or out of his control. Nowhere does he admit fault for his belief in the manipulations of Don Jon or his cruel treatment of his apparent 'love'.

Tasks: Claudio; masculinity; noting; social norms; guilt.

"my brother hath a daughter, almost the copy of my child that's dead, and she alone is heir to both of us: give her the right you should have given her cousin, and so dies my revenge."

Leonato, Act 5, Scene 1

Leonato offers Claudio punishments for his actions. They are to tell all of Messina that Hero is innocent and then to sing a death song for Hero at her grave. The final instruction is the above: to marry Hero's cousin ("Give her the right you should have given her cousin") and Leonato will forgive ("dies my revenge").

But there is no cousin. Leonato's plan is to present Hero behind a veil and, at the last minute, reveal her. This is the final gulling, final manipulation to punish Claudio. This leap of faith will make him 'worthy' to marry Hero and restoring his social standing by being obedient to Leonato and his family's wishes.

Yet, notice that Don Pedro escapes the majority of punishment – he is royalty after all and Leonato is unable to inflict anything upon him. Don Pedro's social standing protects him from the anger of a more minor family. The same cannot be said for Claudio – although he still has the protection of Don Pedro.

It is also interesting to note that Leonato presents this "cousin" as "almost the copy of my child" (i.e. she's beautiful and innocent) and "heir to both of us" (i.e. rich and powerful). Claudio is being asked to marry someone he has never seen, true, but there is little sense of him 'losing' anything in this punishment. He is being asked to make a leap of faith and marry someone he hasn't seen (and may not be attracted to) but the risk to his social standing is minor. Especially when Leonato goes to such pains to say she is rich and beautiful!

It is also interesting to note that this situation allows Leonato's social standing to be restored – Hero and Claudio's marriage will take place. If we are kind, then Hero also gets what she wants (she still loves Claudio) … But she is never asked if this is what she wants! She was the one wronged after all.

Tasks: Claudio; masculinity; gulling; marriage; social norms.

"Sweet Beatrice, wouldst thou come when I called thee?"

Benedick, Act 5, Scene 2

Benedick and Beatrice greet each other. After the revelation of their love for each other, Benedick's language is softer and gentler ("sweet") showing his affection. The use of a question (inviting a response and, therefore, communication and conversation) is different from the clipped and angry 'witty' sentences they exchanged earlier in the play. Notice that his question is also uncertain ("wouldst thou come") reflecting his own uncertainty in these new feelings.

Tasks: romantic love; Benedick; wit.

"tell me for which of my bad parts didst thou first fall in love with me?"

Benedick, Act 5, Scene 2

Beatrice demands assurances that Benedick has challenged Claudio to a duel (which she gets) and then they exchange sweet and silly comments. There is some reflection of the wit and word play used earlier, but now it is directed inwards rather than outwards – Benedick makes fun of himself ("bad parts") and jokes at his own expense, creating a softer mood. This scene sees the intelligence that opened the play on display between these two characters but changed due to these new emotions.

It is interesting to note that Benedick is seeking a kind of reassurance ("didst though first fall in love with me?") that Beatrice truly loves him. This lack of certainty is reflected also in his use of a question. It is possible that he doubts Beatrice's love, perhaps a small doubt that she is manipulating him to use him to fight Claudio. Therefore, he seeks assurances of her love.

This sentence also interestingly acknowledges that he will not be the 'perfect' man or husband (which, for example, Claudio is expected to be) but that "love" is based on "bad parts" also – in seeing the reality of your partner, as these two do of each other.

Tasks: romantic love; Benedick; wit.

"I do suffer love indeed, for I love thee against my will."

Benedick, Act 5, Scene 2

Benedick acknowledges the difficulty he has in expressing and feeling the "love" that has grown between himself and Beatrice. He uses the word choice of "suffer" to show both the process of falling love (being gulled, etc) and the burden of proving his love (having to duel and kill his friend).

The almost **oxymoronic** "suffer love" shows the honest reality of the love between these two, contrasting with the false love sometimes seen in Claudio and Hero. There is something more personal happening here.

Benedick uses the phrase "against my will" to mean against his better judgement, but ironically calls back to the 'gulling' scene to show that he has had little choice in this situation.

Tasks: Benedick; romantic love; deceit.

"Thou and I are too wise to woo peaceably."

Benedick, Act 5, Scene 2

Benedick and Beatrice's conversation in this Scene is not as angry or volatile as earlier conversations but it is still not "peaceably" undertaken, implying that they still irritate each other and there is still a power struggle between the two. Benedick says it is because they are "too wise", meaning their age (both are older than Claudio and Hero), life experience, role in society (both are vague social outsiders), and their innate intelligence 'get in the way' of their own happiness.

Yet, Benedick's tone is almost happy, implying that he sees honesty and truth in this kind of love – these two characters know and 'see' each other, including faults, and this will lead to a more honest and long-lasting happiness.

Notice the pronoun use. Benedick doesn't say "we" – both these characters retain their individuality ("thou" and "I") and sense of self – but he puts Beatrice first ("thou") in the sentence.

Tasks: Benedick; romantic love; noting.

"Well, I am glad that all things sort so well."

Antonio, Act 5, Scene 4

Shakespeare is gearing up to finish the play and give the audience a happy ending – the "much ado" about "nothing" is soon to be sorted. Antonio speaks for the audience in that we are "glad" and happy that the situation will not end in tragedy and the phrase "sort so well" gives a sense of order and stability to the chaos that reigned in the middle of the play. This reflects not just on Don Jon's plan, but also the romantic antics and the 'gulling'/playing. It is time for marriage – and settling down!

Tasks: romantic love; marriage; social norms.

"Re-enter ANTONIO, with the Ladies masked"

Stage Direction, Act 5, Scene 4

All are on the stage here and Claudio must marry Hero's supposed 'cousin' to show his penance. This is the final 'gulling' within the play – that of Claudio, and the society of Messina is about to reassert its social norms. The play ends in a marriage to show that volatility of the romantic and the tragic are coming to end within this society – a period of the domestic is dawning.

It is interesting that the ladies are "masked" – this makes the current situation almost like a play or a performance. It is a ritual moment of playing that allows the tension and violence that existed earlier in the play to finally dissipate.

Yet, interestingly, Claudio is once again experiencing one of his main faults, one that led him into this in the first place – he is showing obscured sight! He doesn't understand, see, or 'note' the events and what is really happening. He is, once again, being tricked. Yet, this time, it is Messina society 'gulling' the young man to bring him – and Hero – back into line. There is a sense that Claudio's lack of true sight is an advantage here rather than the disadvantage and weakness that was being exploited by Don Jon earlier in the play.

Tasks: romantic love; social norms; marriage; noting.

"One Hero died defiled, but I do live,

And surely as I live, I am a maid."

Hero, Act 5, Scene 4

Hero is unmasked as herself and Claudio is suitably shocked – and pleased! He has performed his penance and received his just reward, as well as Hero. They can marry.

Yet the language in the above quotation is interesting in that Hero linguistically doubles herself. She says that "one Hero died" (i.e. the Hero who was perceived to have committed sin) and that this other Hero took the negative reputation to her grave. This idea is emphasised with alliteration, near rhyme and negative word choice ("died defiled").

This is a classic example of a **scape goat**, which is when a society kills (or emulates killing) an animal or person to 'kill' the sins of the community. Despite having done nothing wrong, Hero needed to ritually 'die' to be re-born as 'clean'.

Hero also asserts her 'clean-ness' and suitability for marriage ("I am a maid"). Notice that she does this not just for Claudio but in front of the high born of Messina. Hero is reclaiming her reputation and status as a 'good' woman of the community before she is then accepted as a married woman, taking her place in society as a woman of power and influence.

Tasks: Hero; noting; societal norms.

"'Tis no such matter. Then you do not love me?"

Benedick, Act 5, Scene 4

Benedick calls on Beatrice to unmask herself and demands to know if she loves him. He intends they marry at the same time as Claudio and Hero. His tone is different from earlier and offends Beatrice. They bicker, and the 'gulling' of them is revealed. There is brief moment ("Tis no such matter") when their love may collapse as they both try to save face and reputation, too proud to admit their love publicly ("Then you do not love me?")

Tasks: Beatrice; Benedick; romantic love; reputation.

"Peace! I will stop your mouth."

Benedick, Act 5, Scene 4

Hero and Claudio step in to save Beatrice and Benedick, revealing poems they had written for each other. It is interesting that Hero and Claudio perform this action – these are the two who understand and have lived through the 'traditional' role of man and woman, husband and wife. It is almost as society through them is pushing Beatrice and Benedick together, releasing them from their role as 'wits' (who are only occupied with their reputation and intelligence) to allow them to experience romantic love and happiness.

They both cave very quickly (Shakespeare really wants to tie everything up with a neat bow!) and this reflected in the shortness of the sentences and the use of the exclamation. The exclamation mark also represents the joy Benedick feels in his new love while the word choice of "peace" is interestingly contrasted with the language from earlier: a "merry war" has ended in this marriage and in this "kiss".

The language here also makes it really clear what is 'getting in the way' with these two – "I will stop your mouth". Once again it is language and talking which stops true happiness and love. Their 'wit' and intelligence were fine for their social position as outsiders at the beginning of the play, but to be husband and wife they need to transform their role in society.

Tasks: Beatrice; Benedick; romantic love; reputation.

"'Prince, thou art sad; get thee a wife, get thee a wife"

Benedick, Act 5, Scene 4

Benedick's attitude here contrasts with earlier when he claimed a wife is the last thing a man needs and, in fact, claimed he would never marry. The repetition above shows both his humour but his seriousness, while contrasting "sad" with "wife" implies that domestic happiness balances sadness and loneliness.

Tasks: Benedick; romantic love; marriage.

> *"Think not on him till to-morrow:*
> *I'll devise thee brave punishments for him."*
>
> ### Benedick, Act 5, Scene 4

In the final moments of the play, when peace is finally arrived at, a messenger arrives to tell the characters (and the audience) that Don Jon has been captured. The final thing that could cause disruption to society has been subdued.

Yet, in a play that has a happy ending, some of the final language is around negativity ("think not") and pain ("punishments"). The tragedy that was bristling just under the surface of the play from the beginning comes to the fore again. There is a sense of danger and pain that is not far away in this society.

It is entirely possible that this is just the final piece of the puzzle that Shakespeare wishes to place into the jigsaw to create a 'neat' ending, but one of the final words in the whole play is "him" – a reference to the discontent, the unhappy, the character who has no place and no real role. Don John both rejected (and was rejected by) society and he represents the danger that happens when we do this, when we push people to the sides.

Tasks: Benedick; societal norms; reputation.

> ### *"Dance"*
>
> ### Stage Direction, Act 5, Scene 4

The final lines of the play are Benedick asking for music and the final stage direction is the above. The happy music and movement represent the resolution of the play in happiness. It is the happy ending made flesh on the stage. Interestingly this "dance" would be highly structured, like marriages of the time.

The physical "dance" would also provide entertainment for the audience, a final moment of spectacle as they make their way out of the theatre – a final moment of frivolity to watch these characters enjoy their new happy lives.

Tasks: Benedick; romantic love; marriage.

Writing an essay
Yeah, but how do I write an essay?

Okay, well, let's start with the fact that your teacher has probably taught you some structures already, and you've probably practised it since you were in your first years of senior and/or secondary education! You know how to write an essay – all that knowledge is tucked away in your brain somewhere.

But if you need a little reminder, here's some advice....

Task

The exam paper has a task on it. This is what is going to drive your essay. You should be referring to that task twice in every paragraph of your essay. We usually use the **key word from the task** in the first line and last line of each paragraph.

This is called 'topping and tailing' – it is at the top and tail of each paragraph. This lets the marker know that you are definitely answering the question/doing the task. This is guaranteed to up your mark.

Do not just write all the information that you know. Only write information that is relevant to an appropriate task. For example, if you decide to write about romantic love – why are you talking about Iago's character? You may know about it, but it probably isn't fully relevant! This loses marks.

Introductions

These are not explicitly in most mark schemes (although "structure" usually is and introductions are a point of structure), but they are expected by all markers. They allow the marker to understand the task, text, and approach you are going to take. They set the scene, set up the essay, give the marker the low down, etc. An essay without an introduction just seems odd!

There are standard things introductions contain:

- **Title:** "Much Ado About Nothing"

- **Full name of author:** William Shakespeare

- **Reference to task:** I am going to discuss …

- **Some sort of summary:** This drama is about

Weaker introduction

Task: discuss a drama where there is major theme.

I am going to discuss "Much Ado About Nothing" by William Shakespeare. I am going to talk about the major theme of romantic love that is present in this play. This play is about a group of soldiers who arrange their marriages after they have been at war and have won.

Better introduction

Task: discuss a drama where there is major theme.

William Shakespeare's "Much Ado About Nothing" is a drama where the major theme of romantic love is particularly important to character and narrative. The drama centres around the 'wooing' of Hero for Claudio and Beatrice for Benedick. The men are returning soldiers post-war who enter an 'Eden-like' Messina and try to claim their post-war happiness. The drama follows the political, social, and emotional journeys of these characters to reveal their love to each other and enter the socially acceptable state of marriage by the end of the play.

Analytical paragraphs

These are the paragraphs that make up the **body** of your essay. This is mostly what your marks are going to come from. You need to make sure you have a minimum of three – one from the start, one from the middle and one from the end. This shows coverage. You probably want to work **chronologically** (start to middle to end) rather than out of order.

You may have been taught an acronym (PEA, PEAR, PCQE, etc) for producing these. These systems do work. I am going to speak more generally, and you should see it's the same information I'm telling you – just different terminology.

The standard things included in analytical paragraphs:

- **A literary technique:** The writer uses a pun
- **Reference to the task:** This creates the theme
- **A quotation in " " marks**: "suffer love"
- **Knowledge of the drama**
- **Analysis of the quotation**

Weaker analytical paragraphs

Task: discuss a drama where here there is major theme.

Shakespeare uses a pun, "suffer love". This is from Act 5. This is what Benedick thinks of romantic love. This shows the theme.

Better analytical paragraphs

Task: discuss a drama where here there is major theme.

Shakespeare uses an oxymoronic pun, "suffer love". This is Act 5 Scene 2 where Benedick teases Beatrice about their love which they have revealed to each other. The word "love" shows his true affection, while "suffer" implies (to comedic effect) that "love" is an illness that he is enduring. It also implies that their relationship will be rocky but all the more real and true due to this. This clearly shows the romantic love between the two.

Conclusions

Like, introductions, these are not explicitly in most mark schemes (again "structure" is, and conclusions are a point of structure), and so are expected by markers. They summarise your ideas, round off your essay, give you a last chance to say anything to show a lesson that you have learned.

There are standard things conclusions contain:

- **Concluding phrase:** In conclusion,
- **Repeat title:** "Much Ado About Nothing"
- **Repeat full name of author:** William Shakespeare
- **Reference to task:** I have discussed ...
- **Personal reaction:** I have learned ...

Weaker conclusion

Task: discuss a drama where there is major theme.

In conclusion, I have discussed "Much Ado About Nothing" by William Shakespeare. This drama has an important theme of romantic love which I have talked about in my essay.

Better conclusion

Task: discuss a drama where there is major theme.

In conclusion, William Shakespeare's "Much Ado About Nothing" is a drama which is driven by romantic love. This can be seen in how the 'gulling' scenes are both pivotal for the characters, the narrative, and the theme of romantic love itself. The drama teaches the audience about the fickle nature of appearances and how love must be based on something more grounded and solid than just what we can see – therefore Hero and Claudio's shallow courtly love is contrasted with the more realistic and so lasting love of Beatrice and Benedick. Romantic love, within this play, is also presented as a tool of control by society, a weapon used to create conformity in the outliers such as Beatrice and Benedick.

Disclaimer about the use of exemplars:

Exemplars are useful ways to 'see' what high end essays look like and understand what to sound like when you write your own. It can even be useful to try to memorise parts or ideas from an exemplar to then write in your exam – you have learned them after all!

You fully have my permission to use these exemplars to *inform* your own work, and as revision/learning tools for an exam. That's what they were created for.

But **plagiarism** is never acceptable

This is trying to pass off an exemplar as piece of homework or claiming that you have written it when you did not. Especially when that work forms part of a grade awarded to you by a teacher.

Your teacher will know! Don't be a fool!

Exemplar Essay 1

Discuss a drama with a memorable character (Beatrice).

William Shakespeare's "Much Ado About Nothing" is a drama which centres around the return of soldiers (Don Pedro, Claudio, Benedick) to Messina post-war. Messina, a place of sunshine and happiness, represents a kind of Eden for the men – and the possibility of marriage. The main narrative thrust of the play surrounds the 'wooing' of Hero for Claudio and Beatrice for Benedick, including the famous 'gulling' scenes, where trickery is used to make characters admit their true love for each other. The drama follows the political, social, and emotional journeys of these characters to reveal their love to each other and enter the socially acceptable state of marriage by the end of the play. Beatrice is a central female character within the play, and one who is memorable to the audience both for her intelligence but also for her lack of conformity to the socially accepted standards of femininity of the Shakespearean stage.

Shakespeare uses a metaphor in Act 1 Scene 1 to begin the memorable characterisation of Beatrice, "I pray you, is Signior Mountanto returned from the wars or no?" Before Don Pedro and his soldiers arrive, they are discussed by Leonato and his family. Beatrice's very first line is a question about Benedick to a messenger. The fact that she uses speaks about him almost immediately hints at her desire to know if he is alive and well ("returned from the wars or no"), while the cutting remark that she uses shows the audience her role as a 'wit' (someone who uses their intelligence to make courtly puns and jokes for the amusement of others) She uses a metaphor to describe him: "mountanto". This is a movement in fencing which is seen as over-the-top and a kind of showing off. She is, therefore, call him 'Mr Show-off'. This is a common insult that Beatrice levels towards Benedick, and she somewhat sees her own role in the society of Messina as someone who 'pricks' or destroys the over-inflated egos of the men. This is a role that Beatrice is able to occupy – an unusual status for a woman – due to the fact that she is Leonato's niece and not his heir. Beatrice does not have the societal pressure of other female characters to get married and be the familial heir. Therefore, both her interesting role in society and her role as a wit make her an interesting and memorable character.

The character of Beatrice is developed further in Act 2 Scene 2 through a metaphor, "he lent it me awhile; and I gave him use for it, a double heart for his single one: marry, once before he won it of me with false dice". Here Don Pedro tells Beatrice she has "lost the heart" of Benedick due to her insults, and she responds by telling him about their romantic past. She uses the extended metaphor of physically giving him her "heart" to represent the love and romance that was once between them. Benedick initially proclaimed to love her ("he lent it me") and she returned that love ("a double heart") but he lied to her about his intentions ("false dice"). The physical giving of a "heart" is common romantic love poetry imagery, and this shows that her love was initially honest. She then perverts this common imagery by using the language of games ("won/false dice") to show that Benedick had been playing with her and she hadn't known. Interestingly, this romantic interest linked to a game continues throughout the play: their arguing is often linked to a kind of game or "merry war". This implies that their romantic relationship didn't end (the game never stopped) but it changed into something else – this arguing which they do now. Beatrice's character is made the more interesting through this developed history and backstory given to the audience.

Shakespeare has Beatrice undergo the most dramatic change after the 'gulling' scene, made most obvious in her use of sentence structure, "What fire is in mine ears? Can this be true? Stand I condemn'd for pride and scorn so much? Contempt, farewell! and maiden pride, adieu!" In Act 3 Scene 1, Beatrice undergoes a self-revelation that she loves Benedick, and, in fact, her own "pride" has been standing in the way of her happiness. Beatrice's use of questions shows her confusion at the situation and disbelief, while her use of exclamation marks indicates the strength of her newfound love for Benedick. The shortness of the sentences ironically reflects how quickly Beatrice's opinion of Benedick changes, how short a time it takes for her to love him. The gossip that she overheard is metaphorically described as "fire", implying its warming and/or destructive power that it has had on her heart and her self-image. Beatrice also metaphorically bids goodbye ("adieu/farewell") to her previous "pride and scorn" (i.e. her anti-marriage sentiment). This could also be Beatrice budding "adieu" to her previous role as 'niece' and 'wit' which, in part, allowed her to remain unmarried and not take part in the rituals of romantic love that dominates the life of her cousin Hero. Beatrice is made all the more memorable as a character here for the changes that she undergoes.

For some, the most memorable moment is presented by Shakespeare in a short command in Act 4 Scene 1, "Kill Claudio." After Claudio denounces and rejects Hero, Beatrice finally admits to loving Benedick, but she shows reticence and disbelief. After he says that he will prove it to her, she commands him to "Kill Claudio". This is short, straight forward and almost emotionless. It cannot be argued with or changed, which is different from most of the language used between these characters which is often over-long and overly constructed. The short sentence is unarguable, clear, and full of anger. The word "kill" is also aggressive, destructive, and angry. This shows the depth of Beatrice's fierce loyalty to her cousin, but also her sense of right/wrong and justice. It also shows her manipulative control and power over Benedick that he agrees to challenge his friend to a duel! Here Beatrice's presents as masculine, violent, and fiercely loyal. She seems powerful – and unassailable.

Finally, one of Beatrice's most interesting moments is in the final moments of the play, exemplified by this imagery, "Peace! I will stop your mouth." Once Hero and Claudio in Act 5 Scene 4 have resolved their differences, they step in to save Beatrice and Benedick from calling off their wedding. Hero and Claudio reveal poems Beatrice and Benedick had written for each other. It is interesting that Hero and Claudio perform this action – these are the two who understand and have lived through the 'traditional' role of man and woman, husband, and wife. It is almost as if society is pushing Beatrice and Benedick together, releasing them from their role as 'wits' (who are only occupied with their reputation and intelligence) to allow them to experience romantic love and happiness. The word "peace" used by Benedick is interesting as it represents an end to the "merry war" between the two, but the phrase "I will stop your mouth" could represent the silencing of the figure of Beatrice as she accepts the traditional role of wife that has been presented to her. The 'trouble' that Beatrice represented throughout the play (the challenge to male authority, the lack of a clear social role, and the rejector of men) is subsumed and destroyed in her silencing by Benedick. The man and soldier, her husband, has won the "merry war" and quietens her. A modern audience may find this a troubling ending for such a memorable feminist character, or perhaps we should be grateful for the happiness in this ending that is given to her – she is married to a man that she loves, and matches her wit and intelligence.

In conclusion, William Shakespeare's "Much Ado About Nothing" is a drama in which one of the central characters, Beatrice, is memorable not just for her lone strength of mind and character, her loyalty to her cousin and her own place in society, but also because of the changes and depth of change that the character goes through. Beatrice represents the challenging and powerful woman of Shakespeare, who initially defies and then accepts marriage but only on her terms. Beatrice is a character who challenges male authority while also challenging the sexism of the world that she is presented with, using language and intelligence to create a linguistic space for herself. She is often the character who keeps audiences coming back to this play!

Exemplar Essay 2

Discuss a drama with an important theme (romantic love).

William Shakespeare's "Much Ado About Nothing" is a drama which centres around the return of soldiers (Don Pedro, Claudio, Benedick) to Messina post-war. Messina, a place of sunshine and happiness, represents a kind of Eden for the men – and the possibility of marriage. The main narrative thrust of the play surrounds the 'wooing' of Hero for Claudio and Beatrice for Benedick, including the famous 'gulling' scenes, where trickery is used to make characters admit their true love for each other. The drama follows the political, social, and emotional journeys of these characters to reveal their love to each other and enter the socially acceptable state of marriage by the end of the play. Romantic love is a central theme of this play and is presented by a number of characters and couples to contrasting effect.

Shakespeare opens the play with this theme through the use of metaphor from Beatrice in Act 1 Scene1, "I had rather hear my dog bark at a crow, than a man swear he loves me." Beatrice is an important and well-loved character who immediately dismisses the idea of romantic love and, by extension, the idea of marriage. She states she would "rather hear" an annoying noise ("my dog bark at a crow") than a man proclaims his love for her. This is, of course, hyperbolic, and over-the-top. It is intended to make the crowd surrounding laugh, but it does express a truth that Beatrice believes about herself here: that she is better off without a man and doesn't need one. In this sentence she makes a comparison between "my dog" and "a man" – implying that men are animals and not in control of themselves, like the dog with the crow. It is also interesting she compares two noises: "bark/swear". Here she is implying that a man's proclamation of love is as meaningless and senseless as a dog's "bark" and is something reflexive and not to be trusted. This refusal to marry (or to partake in the 'love' games of a courtly woman) is an unusual and independent statement to make, one that she gets away with as she is not Leonato's heir. Hero, Beatrice's cousin and Leonato's heir, could not say a similar statement. But Hero would not be marrying for romantic love but, instead, for political and social union and cohesion. Beatrice's freedom allows her to dismiss romantic love as beneath her, while romantic love as a tool for creating alliances cannot be denied to Hero. Yet the irony of the statement is not lost on an audience – we are aware that Beatrice's fate is to be married and to be ironically mocked by her own love for Benedick later in the play. Beatrice's statement against love almost narratively guarantees that she will fall in love in the course of the play.

Next, Shakespeare develops this idea into Act 2 Scene 1 using a command, "Daughter, remember what I told you: if the prince do solicit you in that kind, you know your answer." Following Beatrice's ridicule of marriage and refusal to marry (even if only a joke), Leonato instructs Hero that she must accept Don Pedro if he asks ("you know your answer"). He is asserting his masculine and fatherly control over his daughter, who has no choice in this situation ("what I told you"). Romantic love is presented purely as secondary here to the social norms and societal structure that rules Hero's life. The use of pronouns and word order are interesting as Leonato puts himself ("I") at the start of the sentence and Hero and her wishes ("you") towards the end. He also asserts that, despite it being his instruction, it is her ("your") answer and not his. He asserts power and demands she take his will as if it were her own – this is very possessive and controlling. Hero's romantic interest is secondary in this situation and presented as ultimately unimportant

Further in Act 2 Scene 1, Shakespeare then begins to link romantic love to 'gulling', deceit and trickery through the use of imagery, "Here, Claudio, I have wooed in thy name, and fair Hero is won." Don Pedro, the prince, pretended to be Claudio to 'win' Hero for his friend. The use of deceit and masks ("wooed in thy name") has been successful and sets up a major motif (that romantic love is produced through trickery) for the play. Love is therefore set up as a game that is "won", implying once again that love is a game to be played. Hero is also "won" like an object, showing her place and social position as daughter and heir in Messina. It is interesting that the game is played more successfully in this play when others intervene. Hero and Claudio's marriage is arranged very quickly, whilst Benedick and Beatrice have been in an on-off again relationship for a long time because they have no 'help' yet from the wider society of Messina. There is an implication that romantic love between two people is important but should be facilitated/created by wider society – that the blessing of others (especially those above you in the social hierarchy) is required.

Shakespeare emphasises the power of romantic love in Act 3 Scene 2 using a metaphor, "his jesting spirit; which is now crept into a lute-string". Both Benedick and Beatrice have been 'gulled' into loving each other, and Claudio and Don Pedro make fun of a change in Benedick, that he no longer has a "jesting spirit". In fact, Benedick tries to cover it up his unhappy love as just toothache, trying to explain away the change in him that he has promised throughout the play that he will not go through. Benedick has stopped being so aggressive in his 'wit' and making comments against love, a large facet of his personality earlier in the play. Instead Benedick has "crept into a lute-string", meaning that he has started to sigh a lot and write/sing love poems/songs for Beatrice. The other men notice this change and mock him for it, almost revelling in his change and fall from the bachelor he was. His change in Benedick represents the power of romantic love, especially when it is endorsed by society, in changing the fundamental nature of the players. Both Benedick and Beatrice both experience a sense of change and express a discomfort and dislike of this change – it is not an easy process.

Yet Shakespeare does present a danger in this power of romantic love, especially when it is framed by society and societal expectations. Shakespeare uses Claudio to express this using oxymoronic imagery in Act 4 Scene 1, "But fare thee well, most foul, most fair! farewell, thou pure impiety and impious purity!" Claudio has been tricked into believing that Hero has been having an affair and, in his confusion, speaks in a series of oxymorons, contrasting words/phrases that seem to contradict each other. This shows his confusion and the contrast/duality of Hero: the appearance of her as good contrasting with her 'secret' liaisons with men. This inside/outside divide is seen in the contrasting statements: "foul/impiety" referring to her apparent actions while "fair/pure" refer to her beauty and her reputation to the world. But Claudio is 'mis-seeing' the lady, caused by Don Jon. All of that power of romantic love – backed up by the societal pressure to marry and the social norms pressing down on Hero – has been transformed into something negative, dangerous, and equally as powerful. These statements also refer to other plays by Shakespeare that feature romantic love, showing how important they are as a thematic link to Shakespeare. Romeo in *Romeo and Juliet* speaks in similar oxymorons to capture his confusion about love (how something 'good' can cause pain), while oxymorons in *Macbeth* show confusion about the good/bad of the witches who cause chaos. In fact, "foul/fair" are exactly the terms used in *Macbeth* to describe the destructive power of the witches.

Yet, in the final scene of the play, Shakespeare uses repetition to show the importance and stability that romantic love (and marriage) bring to society, "Prince, thou art sad; get thee a wife, get thee a wife". This is Benedick in Act 5 Scene 4, in the final moments of the play. All has worked out to a 'happy' ending and the audience have been treated to two marriages and the capture of the villain, Don Jon. Benedick's attitude here contrasts with earlier when he claimed a "wife" is the last thing a man needs and, in fact, claimed he would never marry. He is now encouraging the prince, Don Pedro, that he needs ("get thee") a "wife" in order to be happy. The use of the word "sad" is interesting and it implies that one-ness/unmarried is an undesired and lonely state. The repetition above shows both Benedick's humour but also his seriousness, while contrasting "sad" with "wife" implies that domestic happiness balances sadness and loneliness. The word "get" is interesting in that it has possessive qualities, showing the continued objectification of women and the commercialisation of wedding/romantic love to some extent. Shakespeare does not seem to be arguing that romantic love is false (how can we claim that when these characters – well Beatrice and Benedick – so clearly love each other?) but a modern audience may have a small warning bell ringing about the pressure exerted by others during romantic love and wooing, and the idea that romantic love must end in marriage to create societal stability. Yet, Shakespeare is still a playwright and so 'happy marriage' is a neat and easy way to round off and end his play, especially the marriage of the confirmed "bachelors" of Benedick and Beatrice.

In conclusion, William Shakespeare's "Much Ado About Nothing" is a drama in which romantic love is a key theme which drives the characters and the narratives. It is a theme which Shakespeare explores with excellent skill and 'wit'. He displays for us the need for romantic love in order to build societal cohesion and stability (as seen through Hero and Claudio's marriage) but also to bring happiness and end loneliness (as seen through Benedick and Beatrice's marriage). Romantic love – and its extension marriage – are social and societal tools, and therefore, as with all tools, must be treated with an element of caution (the denouncing of Hero came very close to ending this play as a tragedy). Yet, romantic love is also the main driving force of that thing beloved by audiences – a happy ending!

Exemplar Essay 3

Discuss a drama with an important relationship (Benedick/Beatrice)

William Shakespeare's "Much Ado About Nothing" is a drama which centres around the return of soldiers (Don Pedro, Claudio, Benedick) to Messina post-war. Messina, a place of sunshine and happiness, represents a kind of Eden for the men – and the possibility of marriage. The main narrative thrust of the play surrounds the 'wooing' of Hero for Claudio and Beatrice for Benedick, including the famous 'gulling' scenes, where trickery is used to make characters admit their true love for each other. The drama follows the political, social, and emotional journeys of these characters to reveal their love to each other and enter the socially acceptable state of marriage by the end of the play. Beatrice and Benedick are two central characters within this play who start of as 'wits' and misfits within society – claiming they will never marry – but end the play as a couple married couple, truly in love and devoted. This relationship is important both narratively and thematically to the play.

Shakespeare uses a metaphor in Act 1 Scene 1 to begin the important relationship "I pray you, is Signior Mountanto returned from the wars or no?" Before Don Pedro and his soldiers arrive, they are discussed by Leonato and his family. Beatrice's very first line is a question about Benedick to a messenger. The fact that she uses speaks about him almost immediately hints at her desire to know if he is alive and well ("returned from the wars or no"), while the cutting remark that she uses shows the audience her role as a 'wit' (someone who uses their intelligence to make courtly puns and jokes for the amusement of others) She uses a metaphor to describe him: "mountanto". This is a movement in fencing which is seen as over-the-top and a kind of showing off. She is, therefore, call him 'Mr Show-off'. This is a common insult that Beatrice levels towards Benedick, and she somewhat sees her own role in the society of Messina as someone who 'pricks' or destroys the over-inflated egos of the men. Yet the use of the two B-beginning names (Benedick, Beatrice) immediately links these two characters for the audience, hinting that they are destined to be together. It is also interesting that Beatrice chooses a fencing metaphor – because fencing is something done with an equal partner! The implication, of course, is that Beatrice sees him as both a partner and an equal and, therefore, already considers him a worth match for marrying. Shakespeare seems to be showing us their compatibility as a couple when we look behind the thin veneer of anger that seems to exist.

The relationship is developed further in Act 2 Scene 2 through a metaphor, "he lent it me awhile; and I gave him use for it, a double heart for his single one: marry, once before he won it of me with false dice". Here Don Pedro tells Beatrice she has "lost the heart" of Benedick due to her insults, and she responds by telling him about their romantic past. She uses the extended metaphor of physically giving him her "heart" to represent the love and romance that was once between them. Benedick initially proclaimed to love her ("he lent it me") and she returned that love ("a double heart") but he lied to her about his intentions ("false dice"). The physical giving of a "heart" is common romantic love poetry imagery, and this shows that her love was initially honest. She then perverts this common imagery by using the language of games ("won/false dice") to show that Benedick had been playing with her and she hadn't known. Interestingly, this romantic interest linked to a game continues throughout the play: their arguing is often linked to a kind of game or "merry war". This implies that their romantic relationship didn't end (the game never stopped) but it changed into something else – this arguing which they do now. The relationship is shown to be more complex than the initially bickering showed us, hinting to the audience of deeper feelings (both love and hurt) that have existed for a long time. It also adds a melancholy edge of Beatrice's swearing off marriage (she was hurt before) and Benedick's masculine bravado (perhaps he was too young/too much of a solider to express himself).

Shakespeare develops this relationship into romantic love after the 'gulling' scenes, made most obvious in Leonato's imagery in Act 2 Scene 3, "she loves him with an enraged affection". This is the gulling of Benedick, but a similar trick is used on Beatrice. Leonato pretends that Beatrice "loves" Benedick, loud enough for him to overhear. This is both a narrative (moves the plot along) and comic moment – the men (Leonato, Don Pedro, etc) are meant to be speaking so loudly and slowly to be heard that is obvious they are tricking Benedick. The same is true of Beatrice and her gulling by Hero and company. But Benedick (and Beatrice) are so desperate to hear this (because it is secretly what they want to hear), they ignore how obvious the trick is. They want to be gulled; they want to be tricked. Trickery, like the masks used elsewhere in this play, allow the revelation of some truth. Notice that Leonato intertwines the idea of passion ("loves/affection") with anger ("enraged"). This is how they build up the idea of Beatrice hiding her love for Benedick behind her anger then whenever she shouts him it is because she loves him and is frustrated not to have him ("past the infinite of thought"). Benedick takes this to mean that Beatrice's disdain and dislike are a sign of her love. It is interesting that Leonato has noticed (consciously or note) that the anger between these two, the passion, is driven from a place of love – either love that used to exist or is still present beneath the 'witty' arguing. Shakespeare here cleverly inverts and reverses the signs and symbols of love and anger – the become their own opposites.

For some, the most memorable moment in this relationship is presented by Shakespeare in a short command in Act 4 Scene 1, "Kill Claudio." After Claudio denounces and rejects Hero, Beatrice finally admits to loving Benedick, but she shows reticence and disbelief. After he says that he will prove it to her, she commands him to "Kill Claudio". This is short, straight forward and almost emotionless. It cannot be argued with or changed, which is different from most of the language used between these characters which is often over-long and overly constructed. The short sentence is unarguable, clear, and full of anger. The word "kill" is also aggressive, destructive, and angry. This shows the depth of Beatrice's fierce loyalty to her cousin, but also her sense of right/wrong and justice. It also shows her manipulative control and power over Benedick that he agrees to challenge his friend to a duel! Here Beatrice's presents as masculine, violent, and fiercely loyal. She seems powerful – and unassailable. The combination of Benedick's soldierly skill and Beatrice's powerful will and mind makes a deadly combination here, one that could potentially move the play into the arena of a tragedy. It also clearly shows us the controlling partner in this relationship, with an interesting dynamic which many maybe would not have expected from a drama from this time period – clearly Beatrice, the woman, is in charge here.

Finally, the relationship is rounded up in the final act by Shakespeare by the use of imagery, "Peace! I will stop your mouth." Once Hero and Claudio in Act 5 Scene 4 have resolved their differences, they step in to save Beatrice and Benedick from calling off their wedding. Hero and Claudio reveal poems Beatrice and Benedick had written for each other and so allow them to freely admit their love, breaking through their facades of carelessness. It is interesting that Hero and Claudio perform this action – these are the two who understand and have lived through the 'traditional' role of man and woman, husband and wife. It is almost as if society is pushing Beatrice and Benedick together, releasing them from their role as 'wits' (who are only occupied with their reputation and intelligence) to allow them to experience romantic love and happiness. The word "peace" used by Benedick is interesting as it represents an end to the "merry war" between the two, but the phrase "I will stop your mouth" could represent the silencing of the figure of Beatrice as she accepts the traditional role of wife that has been presented to her. The 'trouble' that Beatrice represented throughout the play (the challenge to male authority, the lack of a clear social role, and the rejector of men) is subsumed and destroyed in her silencing by Benedick. The man and soldier, her husband, has won the "merry war" and quietens her. A modern audience may find this a troubling ending for such a memorable feminist character, or perhaps we should be grateful for the happiness in this ending that is given to her – she is married to a man that she loves, and matches her wit and intelligence.

In conclusion, William Shakespeare's "Much Ado About Nothing" is a drama in which the two central characters, Beatrice and Benedick, are remembered for their wit and their intelligence. But the narrative journey that they go through – from misfits and outsiders at the beginning to then become a married and socially accepted couple – represents the narrative arc of the whole play from chaos to stability, from loneliness to marriage. But, unlike Hero and Claudio whose love seems rather farcical and facile, Benedick and Beatrice's relationship (shown by their history, their reticence to admit their feelings, and their unusual power dynamic) seems more realistic and therefore destined to last the course. They truly have a happy ending.

Exemplar Essay 4

Discuss a drama which has a climax or a turning point.

William Shakespeare's "Much Ado About Nothing" is a drama which centres around the return of soldiers (Don Pedro, Claudio, Benedick) to Messina post-war. Messina, a place of sunshine and happiness, represents a kind of Eden for the men – and the possibility of marriage. The main narrative thrust of the play surrounds the 'wooing' of Hero for Claudio and Beatrice for Benedick, including the famous 'gulling' scenes, where trickery is used to make characters admit their true love for each other. The drama follows the political, social, and emotional journeys of these characters to reveal their love to each other and enter the socially acceptable state of marriage by the end of the play. The main turning point or climax to this narrative is the denouncement of Hero by Claudio, representing the climax of Don Jon's plan. This is particularly important because it represents the moment where the comedy (with a happy ending) could tip into become a tragedy.

First, Shakespeare establishes this plotting arc and begins to set up the climax in Act 1 Scene 1 using an oxymoronic metaphor, "There is a kind of merry war betwixt Signior Benedick and her". On the arrival of all characters to the stage, Beatrice thoroughly ridicules Benedick and Leonato attempts to excuse his niece's seeming hostility with the above statement. He uses the oxymoron of "merry war" to describe the interactions between Beatrice and Benedick. The word "merry" encapsulates the humour in the war of wits for the onlookers, but also seems to imply that the two people themselves enjoy their arguments. Yet the word "war" has implications of violence and destruction, showing that they have the true capability of hurting the other with their words. The word "war" also has implications of a winner, which usually seems to be Beatrice as she is the faster and smarter of the two, but Benedick is a soldier and used to winning "war" so implies the violence and danger of the soldierly arena. Ultimately Shakespeare is also establishing the main narrative tension for the movement of the play: the clash between the "merry" (the humour, jokes, gulling and romance) with the "war" (humiliation, villainy, public denouncement and potential duelling). Shakespeare establishes the climax, the moment where these two things overtake each other later in the play, in this opening line.

Shakespeare develops the narrative in the first half using imagery, "Here, Claudio, I have wooed in thy name, and fair Hero is won." Don Pedro, the prince, pretended to be Claudio to 'win' Hero. The first half of the play is dominated by deceit and masks ("wooed in thy name") to set up the major theme and narrative movement of romance and comedy. Love is set up as a game that is to be played bv all of society – even Benedick and Beatrice who try to opt out. Hero is also "won" like an object, showing her social position in Messina as an heir rather than an individual with personally choice. It is interesting that the game is played more successfully when others intervene: Hero and Claudio's marriage is arranged quickly by Leonato and Don Pedro, whilst Benedick and Beatrice have been in an on-off relationship for a long time because they have had no 'help' from wider society of Messina. Shakespeare is here establishing the narrative of the first half strongly (romance and comedy, gulling and playing) but there are still elements that might make the audience feel discomfort: the machinations of Don Jon and the use of deceit to win love. There is the potential for this to go wrong – which is what is exploited by Shakespeare during the climax.

This potential for the romantic comedy to go wrong takes place in the climax of the wedding scene in Act 4, which is presented by Shakespeare in a metaphor, "Give not this rotten orange to your friend; she's but the sign and semblance of her honour." Don Jon, the villain, convinces Claudio that Hero has cheated on him and, at the altar in front of Messina, Claudio rejects her and accuses her of being unfit for marriage. Claudio implies Hero is an object to be owned and thrown away ("orange"), but this metaphor also has connotations of being spoiled ("rotten") due to her apparent sexual infidelity. Notice that Claudio puts the male-male relationship between himself and Leonato ("your friend") above that of Leonato's with his own daughter. The idea in this sentence is that the masculine world of Messina is dominated by peer-to-peer relationships and that Hero's position is lesser, even if she is family. Claudio is shown to be someone with 'poor' sight/judgement as he confuses Don Jon's lies with truth – he sees Hero's "honour" as a lie ("sign and semblance") rather than the truth it is. This is a sign of Claudio's naivety but also a sign of his misogyny (he believes these lies about Hero very quickly). Claudio's reputation is also reliant upon his masculinity: he is terrified of being humiliated by Hero. This is the climax of the play and the moment when romance is replaced by jealousy and possibly death and destruction.

An immediate effect of this change in the play is presented by Shakespeare in a short command in Act 4 Scene 1, "Kill Claudio." After Claudio denounces and rejects Hero, Beatrice finally admits to loving Benedick, but she demands he prove his love in by duelling with Claudio to the death. This is short, straight forward and almost emotionless; it cannot be argued with or changed, which is different from most of the language used between these characters which is often over-long and overly constructed. The word "kill" is aggressive, destructive, and angry to show the depth of Beatrice's fierce loyalty to her cousin, but also her sense of right/wrong and justice. It also shows her manipulative control and power over Benedick that he agrees to this. Don Jon's plan – and Claudio's naivety and poor judgement – lead to Beatrice's anger. Danger and threat has entered the world of the play now.

Yet the narrative threat in the climax dissipates quickly in Act 5 as Shakespeare uses word choice to wrap up the play, "Don John your brother incensed me to slander the Lady Hero". The plot of Don Jon is revealed by one of his henchmen, Borachio, to Claudio and Don Pedro. The tension of the potential duels dissipates at this revelation and Hero's innocence is sealed ("slander") without a doubt. All see the situation clearly now (it has been spelled out for them!). The next steps of Claudio and Don Pedro can now result in a positive ending – if they can calm down Benedick! The power and narrative weight of this play as a tragedy collapses – with all the violence and anger beginning to be resolved very quickly. Shakespeare does not seem to wish this play to be 'exciting' for very long – there is only the barest threat of the climax/turning point deeply affecting Messina and these characters. There was a brief period where it seemed that it could all go wrong, ending in even more death and destruction, but the intervention of the comic police officers allows a route out of this tragedy and back to the comedy it started as.

In fact, by the end of Act 5, the stage directions make it clear what kind of play 'Much Ado About Nothing' is, "Dance". The final lines of the play are Benedick asking for music and the final stage direction is the above. The audience were held in suspense for a few moments, believing there might be duels and violence, but instead get two marriages, the arrest of the villain and a big "dance" scene to end the play. The happy music and movement represent the resolution of the play in happiness: it is the happy ending made flesh on the stage. Interestingly this "dance" would be highly structured, like marriages of the time, and directors can make many decisions in the staging of this play to allow interactions between characters and even the audience. This can sometimes even be presented almost 'pantomine' like in some productions, to emphasise the ending of the play as a comedy and not as a tragedy in any manner. The physical "dance" would also provide entertainment for the audience, a final moment of spectacle as they make their way out of the theatre – a final moment of frivolity to watch these characters enjoy their new happy lives. The climax has been truly thwarted and put to bed in these last few moments of the narrative.

In conclusion, William Shakespeare's "Much Ado About Nothing" is a drama in which there is an important turning point and climax, but not quite the kind of climax that some audiences are used to. The play sets itself up as a romance – with wit and humour – but the climax represents the potential collapse of this narrative. The Eden-like world of Messina, and the blessed lives of the characters, are corrupted by the machinations of Don Jon and the climax (the denouncement of Hero) represents the potential shift of genre of the entire play from comedy to tragedy, allowing anger, violence and death to enter this stage-world. Yet, this climax dissipates quickly and Shakespeare quickly 'course corrects' and brings the happy endings back into focus. This creates a complex narrative and set of characters from what is sometimes dubbed a 'rom-com' style play from Shakespeare – but which is actually something much more than that thanks to this pivotal moment!

Exemplar Essay 5

Discuss a drama with an important theme (noting or seeing).

William Shakespeare's "Much Ado About Nothing" is a drama which centres around the return of soldiers (Don Pedro, Claudio, Benedick) to Messina post-war. Messina, a place of sunshine and happiness, represents a kind of Eden for the men – and the possibility of marriage. The main narrative thrust of the play surrounds the 'wooing' of Hero for Claudio and Beatrice for Benedick, including the famous 'gulling' scenes, where trickery is used to make characters admit their true love for each other. The drama follows the political, social, and emotional journeys of these characters to reveal their love to each other and enter the socially acceptable state of marriage by the end of the play. Noting or seeing is a major theme which drives the narrative and characters of this play, both the ability to see clearly and its opposite: the naively or lack of clarity in seeing others. This is made much more complicated by the use of masks, gulling and trickery: who can see behind and through facades?

Our starting point is actually the title of the play itself: "Much Ado About Nothing". The phrase "Much Ado" means a lot of discussion or problems, yet the word "ado" has connotations of frivolous or unreal problems. "Much Ado" is very similar to the British phrase of 'a big fuss' or lots of bother over nothing.

This sets the comedic and unreal tone very the beginning – the problems that are generated within this play are not real. The word "nothing" has multiple meanings to be examined. Firstly, "nothing" in Shakespeare's time would have been pronounced identically to "noting". This is a word that means to see or understanding clearly. Therefore, the play title can be referred to as *Much Ado About Seeing*, which is exactly what happens in the play! People seeing each other causes "much ado" or a fuss – both in the sense that people literally see each other (like Benedick and Beatrice spying on others) or in the sense of seeing each other truly (i.e. Claudio is unable to 'note' Hero correctly and therefore causes problems). This clearly establishes the theme we are discussing. Yet, "nothing" also implies that the problems that seem real in this play are not and that the characters are making a 'fuss', which turns out to be literally true since, for the most part, many of the problems are both made up and never cause anyone any real danger. They are "nothing" in the sense of not existing and "nothing" in the sense that they do not cause any real or lasting trouble. This further establishes the comedic tone that is important to the entire play.

Shakespeare establishes the theme of seeing immediately using an insult, "I wonder that you will still be talking, Signior Benedick: nobody marks you.". This is Beatrice's response in Act 1 to one of Benedick's silly jokes (that Leonato cannot be Hero's father as she is too pretty). Beatrice is defending her uncle, but also there is a sense of jealousy that she is not the centre of attention (Benedick is being the 'funny' one). Beatrice wishes to be seen and hold the attention of every-one so uses her wit and humour to 'steal' the spotlight from Benedick. She says that no-one pays attention to him ("nobody marks you") implying that he is not worthy of attention or is just silly. This is a very forthright attack on his honour, which she is able to get away with due to the "merry war". She is also further saying that nobody sees him in the same way that she does – no-one realises that he is a fraud but that she does. Beatrice is implying that she has clear sight, especially when it comes to understanding Benedick. The idea of who can see 'clearly' is important throughout, especially when it comes to Don Jon's plans.

Shakespeare develops this theme using the 'gulling' scenes in Act 2 and 3 and, specifically, through the use of imagery, "By this day! she's a fair lady: I do spy some marks of love in her." After being 'gulled', Beatrice and Benedick very quickly change their opinions of each other and claim to love each other. In this line, Benedick describes looking at Beatrice who is walking across to get him. He appreciates her beauty ("she's a fair lady") but also acknowledges that she is smart and funny – he is 'seeing' her as others have now. It is possible that he has just fallen in love with her, but it seems more likely that the 'gulling' of Benedick (and Beatrice) has cleared their vision of each other and allowed them to 'see' that they are a perfect match. What is interesting in the above quotation is that Benedick believes that Beatrice's angry expression is "some marks of love". This is one of many examples of inversion: where things mean their opposites or look their opposites. In this case, Benedick thinks that Beatrice's open hostility and dislike in her facial expression indicates the depth of her love for him. Shakespeare, here, has layered the 'noting': Benedick can finally 'see' Beatrice for the beautiful and intelligent woman that she is, but he doesn't actually 'see' her properly when he looks at her (he thinks she is in love when she is angry). This irony is created by the gulling, which inverts clear sight to create love.

Yet seeing and mis-seeing also has a dark side, presented in a metaphor in Act 4 by Shakespeare, "Give not this rotten orange to your friend; she's but the sign and semblance of her honour." Don Jon, the villain, convinces Claudio that Hero has cheated on him and, at the altar in front of Messina, Claudio rejects her and accuses her of being unfit for marriage. Claudio implies Hero is an object to be owned and thrown away ("orange"), but this metaphor also has connotations of being spoiled ("rotten") due to her apparent sexual infidelity. Notice that Claudio puts the male-male relationship between himself and Leonato ("your friend") above that of Leonato's with his own daughter. The idea in this sentence is that the masculine world of Messina is dominated by peer-to-peer relationships and that Hero's position is lesser, even if she is family. Claudio is shown to be someone with 'poor' sight/judgement as he confuses Don

85

Jon's lies with truth – he sees Hero's "honour" as a lie ("sign and semblance") rather than the truth it is. This is a sign of Claudio's naivety but also a sign of his misogyny (he believes these lies about Hero very quickly). Claudio's reputation is also reliant upon his masculinity: he is terrified of being humiliated by Hero. Claudio's poor sight – and Don Jon's manipulation of perceptions – allows violence and danger to enter the perfect world of Eden-like Messina. This highlights its importance.

Shakespeare contrasts Claudio's poor sight with Beatrice's good sight through the use of an exclamation, "O, on my soul, my cousin is belied!" Beatrice defends her cousin instantly. Her strength of feeling can be seen in the sentence structure beginning with the "O" and ending in an exclamation mark. The depth of her feeling and trust can be seen in her language ("on my soul"), showing her certainty. Beatrice can 'see' correctly and may not be able to understand exactly what happened but knows it is wrong. It is interesting that Beatrice describes Hero as "belied". The construction of this verb makes the lie seem like an assault or violence with the suffix of be-meaning 'around, from all sides'. This creates an image of Hero as being surrounded by lies, and Beatrice immediately 'sees' the violence being perpetrated. Beatrice's strong defence of her cousin – and her rejection of the men's claims against her – show her unusual status within Leonato's household. Hero barely defends herself, but Beatrice shows many masculine qualities within her defence. She is rejecting the idea of being a meek and quiet woman. Beatrice sees the truth clearly and the exclamation represents the violence that mis-seeing brings into the play.

The correction of poor sight is the key to the resolution of the play, which Shakespeare presents in the use of verbs: "yet sinn'd I not but in mistaking". Claudio and Don Pedro both apologise to Leonato for their role in the 'death' of Hero and offer penance – but they do it with the caveat that they didn't really know that they were doing anything wrong. They claim it was an honest mistake – caused by poor sight and mis-seeing the situation. Notice that Claudio frames his crime has "sinn'd I not" – the evil or the deliberate violence towards Hero was not his fault. It wasn't a "sin" that he committed in the religious or criminal sense, merely a mistake. Claudio does not acknowledge the cruel and public way he humiliated Hero and, instead, uses the situation as a form of absolution from his role in events. Claudio positions his humiliation and 'murder' of Hero as a result of "mistaking" – misunderstanding, mis-seeing and a mistake. All of these remove guilt and blame from him, instead making the situation seem like an accident or out of his control. Nowhere does he admit fault for his belief in the manipulations of Don Jon or his cruel treatment of his apparent 'love'. Yet by correcting his vision, by no longer "mistaking" Hero, Claudio can now return to society and offer Hero a place back from her supposed death. Good sight reinvigorates their love.

Shakespeare finishes on this idea of seeing and pure sight using imagery in Act 5, "One Hero died defiled, but I do live, and surely as I live, I am a maid." Hero is unmasked as herself (the last mask removed in the play) and everyone can finally see her (and each other) for their true selves. Claudio is suitably shocked – and pleased! He has performed his penance and received his just reward, as well as Hero. They can marry. Yet the language in the above quotation is interesting in that Hero linguistically doubles herself. She says that "one Hero died" (i.e. the Hero who was perceived to have committed sin) and that this other Hero took the negative reputation to her grave. This idea is emphasised with alliteration, near rhyme and negative word choice ("died defiled"). This is a classic example of a scape goat, which is when a society kills (or emulates killing) an animal or person to 'kill' the sins of the community. Despite having done nothing wrong, Hero needed to ritually 'die' to be re-born as 'clean' so she can be 'seen' as good again. Hero also asserts her 'clean-ness' and suitability for marriage ("I am a maid"). Notice that she does this not just for Claudio but in front of the high born of Messina. Hero is reclaiming her reputation and status as a 'good' woman of the community before she is then accepted as a married woman, taking her place in society as a woman of power and influence. Hero is demanding to be seen for the good person that she is – and this new 'seeing' allows a happy ending for all in the world of Messina.

In conclusion, William Shakespeare's "Much Ado About Nothing" is a drama in which there is an important theme – that of seeing, noting and sight. Much of the narrative of this play is driven by seeing and spying, for example the gulling, as well as the character development, for example the changes that take place in Claudio when he learns to 'see' correctly. Shakespeare is sending a clear message to the audience about the power of perception and the volatility of sight – and how susceptible we are to distortions, lies, deceit and masks. Shakespeare presents a happy ending for all in Messina – but there was a pivotal moment in the centre where poor sight and noting could have led to disaster and tragedy. Part of "Much Ado About Nothing" is presented as a warning – to see clearly.

Printed in Great Britain
by Amazon

76152731R00058